I0162229

SEPARATE AND SUCCINCT

DISPARATE AND DISTINCT

Poems by
Bill Snider

Separate and Succinct
Disparate and Distinct

Poems by
Bill Snider
2nd Edition 2018
1st Edition Trade Paperback 2014

All Rights Reserved

Dark Recesses Press
657 Craigen Road
Newburgh, Ontario
Canada K0K 2S0

Copyright © 2014 Bill Snider

This is a collection of works of fictitious poetry. Any resemblance to place, person or event is strictly coincidental. All rights reserved.

No part of this book may be reproduced by any means without express written consent, with the exception of small excerpts in print or spoken media for the purpose of review and/or promotion of the entire collection.

Edited by Jodi Lee
Cover Art by Dan Galli
https://www.behance.net/Daniel_Galli

ISBN: 978-1-9888370-3-1

ALSO BY BILL SNIDER

As Zombie Zak

Chaptered and Versed:
Poetic and Cursed
(Twisted Library Press)

Acknowledgments

Michael West (*aka Dr. Pus*) - for kicking me in the backside (figuratively, that is) and making me feel awesome about putting some of my dark poetry out there.

Greg Hall - for being a friendly little funky freakazoid that has always been supportive of my lyrical works.

Matt Devall - for being a stand up person, whom I call friend.

Janet and Chris Morris - for being really cool and helpful!

Mom, Dad, brother Craig and Jason - family is always an important part of life!

And for everybody else who has ever read a word that I've written in conjunction with anything Bright, this is for you: Enjoy, and trek with cookies through the night!

T&ABLE& OF &ONTE&NTS

MONSTERS

MADNESS

MAYHEM

MORE

INTRODUCTION

Dreaming the red, red rain with Bill Snider

Bill Snider writes darkly humorous whispers for the modern ear: evocative poetry and often lyrical prose on grim and fantastical subjects. He writes of monsters, red rain, fearful twilight, dark days and darker nights; he hunts the darkness within himself, and within each reader. And he finds it. Every time. Within this book are eighty poems of, as Bill says, 'monsters, madness, mayhem and more.' The poems are often compelling, sometimes blackly funny, never stilted or verbose, and often chilling. These story poems take you where you've never been before, inside the heart of darkness where a carnival is underway.

Bill, sometimes called Zee by his friends and sometimes Zombie Zak, can write. He writes of creatures and creepers and dark souls in modern breasts that are, as Bill says, "dreaming the red, red rain." Yet this book is not some brooding adolescent recasting of Poe, not merely a modern gothic. Bill is a true original. Humor and horror have equal billing here, sparkling in rhyme and rhythm, and a playfulness that manages never to be at odds with its subjects, who often are zombies and creatures much, much worse.

Bill's poetry takes the dark world of the imagination apart with playful might. Whence this modern poet of the post-modern macabre? Perhaps he's escaped from some dimension akin to ours, so comfortable is he with the inner souls of grim creatures and tortured souls. "I often wonder what it would be like/If I could give up this ability to feel" begins his poem "Man Made Thing."

In the second decade of the twenty-first century, writers and readers are starting to talk of "grimdark" works, works where deepest depths of horrifics are plumbed and stirred and to brew Dantean entertainment. Are Snider's poems grimdark? Some would say yes; and yet the humor in this writer, his empathy for his subjects, his ability to propel you into the minds of creatures that never lived and never will and make them real, and make them friends, is unique in my experience and makes his work stand alone. Zee's voice is solitary; he is the sole proprietor of a very special world of intimate and playful horror. If you open this book and begin to read, you'll be there in a flash.

These poems are often stories: "Liquid Songs" is heroic fantasy and begins "Beneath the surface calm, the trouble boils/ Simmering anger, as the beasts slowly coil." Sometimes, he exalts the ancient myths, sometimes the modern sensibility. In "Under Wraps," Snider begins "Explain this gravity to me:/ What matter of import?/ What Matter of Transport? How is it that this vessel/ Has become so entombed?" If you read on, you find out, and meet a prince and share his fate...

No subject of horror movies or legend or myth is safe from Snider: he remakes them all, and makes them our friends.

By now you've realized I can't and won't categorize this writer; he is a true original, full of love for legends modern and ancient, full of sympathy for monsters and their kin. Snider's prosody is inspired, accessible, distinctive.

Since you have this collection in your hands, waste no more time with me: read on, and enjoy this theme park for the mind that Snider has built for your dark heart and brooding pleasure.

Janet Morris
Author, *The Sacred Band*
Creator, *Heroes in Hell* series

MONSTERS

MONSTER

What monster a man would be that does not wear the mantle of
life?
What mean spirit lurks within the child that does not play in the
living?

Species and doubt are the weapons of the fallen souls that
precede the present.
Finality warped by a lack of exposure to the basic experiences
taken for granted.
Perverse the coil that speeds towards doom consuming those
who fear its embrace
A tortured jacket that we name being a part of the common
weal, in society's grace.

In deepest dread are we who play at godhood eternally blind to
our fears.
Blind are we who sit in judgment of the past and all that is
possibly written.

Balanced by the vagaries of injustice, thwarted by a natural
desire to prey.
Goals that are set and distractions that are chosen and followed
spill outward
Scattered like the spray from a bloodied ricochet, an exit wound
cascade.
Some they are the font of beauty, some the horrors that we hope
will fade.

The sun, to its own merriment shines upon the land of wonder
and splendour
And moon, twin therein spits out just as much for half the work
down under.
Darkness is a weave that grips the deepest places amongst the
souls of all,

The young and old, the weak and strong are all targets for its
dire sights.
A centrefold of destruction and grace that marks the perdition
that waits
For hunger and for temptation, the seeds of want, born of
enmity and hate.

The song it is old and grows quiet moment by moment until
stillness reigns.
The dance it is broken and the manuscript weeps in knowing
that it is done.

Deep down amongst the coals of the spirit of one man, of people
many
Chaos awakens and stirs up the old, the new, the dark and the
bitter bright.
Silently and without foundation, without form, a shadow of
malicious doubt
Stalking the prey that is man's darkest decay, his want, his fears,
his greed.

Without wanting, the essence of being is always close to the
storm centre.
Beyond need, the truth of existence is made barren by the
circumstances.

Beneath the veil of want, tendrils of desire that twist within the
darkened mind
Enveloped within the dream of inescapable need, the lack of
control clear.
Entranced by pinpoints of relevance and dictatorial construct,
social compact
Graced by temperance and villainy that runs afoul of simple
certainty.

With greater and greater confidence, the end arrives too soon,
too soon.
Will there be another beginning? Or is that the final doom once
anon?

Soon, we shall see, the meaning of it all times three.

ONE TERROR TO BLIND THEM

In the eye of my mind, where I keep my monsters
The mystery of existence long forgotten, buried.
Deep within those bowels of dream and memory,
There lies the moist gloaming, of a summer's eve
Where the mysteries of possibility gathered
And discussed what manner of beings were these.
Their visages woven of something possibly broken
Mayhap even deliberately disturbed when woken.
These creatures could wear the beguiling guises
Of friends, of foes, of even those the most nicest.
Deadly enemies of man and beast these were
Their perfidy spread across the land and clear.
Mayhem, merriment, the abandonment of order
Spreading like oily sacrilege within the sacrament.
These beasts could know no honor, or benign love
But by God, we should surely have taken off the gloves.
Let he who hath understanding, reckon upon their gaze
As their fear darkened souls hearken through the haze.
Each moment that we let them stir within the shadows
Is one more day they take back from the daylight gallows.
I've opened up my mind, more fully to understand them.
I regret this move, as now they're both leaf and stem.
Working their way through the land of the living
Terror, fear, death is what they're most giving.

CREEP – (CREEPY CRAWLIES)

We creep, we creep, especially when you sleep!
Through crack and crevice and floorboards deep
We come at you from every angle through and through.
We're the creatures beneath your feet!

We creep, we creep, while all you creatures weep!
For the loss of life, we linger furry, eating cheap
Dinning on the flesh of all things present and fallen
We're the creatures crawling through the walls!

We creep, we creep, exquisitely, we harvest, we reap!
All forms of life we dine upon, fast, slow, you're all sheep
Cattle from which we cull our young, and feed heartily.
We're the creatures sifting through the rubble!

We creep, we creep, throughout the land, this keep!
No construct of man or beast is sufficient against us
All manner of worlds do we find ourselves driven.
We're the creatures through history that have striven!

We creep, we creep, emotions run thick, run deep.
And still we're there at the end, yours, theirs, all,
Feeding upon the remains of the once living.
We're the creatures that will always be unforgiving.

We creep, we creep, and still we creep again!

RED RED RAIN

We search the night, as we hunt for the red, red rain.
The taste, the texture, that salty syrupy decadent sin.
What more this love of the blood that cavorts within
Our souls, our goals, our mission statements?
We sleep the day, always dreaming the red, red rain.
No amount of chaos or perfidy wakens our dark rest
Deep within the embrace of the cool earthen breast
Lay we as we dream the twilight's cursed refrain.
Dark the night, we hunt this way, the red, red rain.
Seek the fleshy things that feed our needs, our ways
Nothing but cattle in our pursuit of fulfilling days
And from so many choices, there are few to complain.
Bright the day, we stay away pining the red, red rain.
Patience, that of the grave, our plaything as we wait
Just out of the comfort zone of prey on a play date.
Soon we launch, soon we hunt, soon we spread pain.
Life, glorified in red rain and blood curdling screams
Essential nutrients, the fulfillment of deadly dreams.
We hunt the night, we stay away through the days
And the cattle know how wicked, how wicked our ways.

MEAT

Oh my sir; what big claws you have!
Dirty, sharpened knifelike talons of rage,
Efficient tools of bestial predation.
>Of course, my dear, the better to rend
>Flesh from bone, stripping clean the prey
>We hunt, we feed it is our imperative.
Oh my, sir; what big teeth you have!
Sharp incisors no doubt that I see,
Shinning and dripping, ready to feed.
>Of course, my dear, the better to eat you
>To fill my gullet fresh and full of warmth
>The dinner is best when full of splatter.
Oh my sir; is that all we are to you?
Fodder for the engine of thy anger, thy need?
Nothing aught save food, sir; naught more?
>Of course, my dear, as prey to predator
>You are the source of our sustenance
>The thing we complete - mmmm, MEAT!

MAN MADE THING

I often wonder what it would be like
If I could give up this ability to feel.
To waltz through life unnatural as it is
Without a care, a hindrance - a semi state of bliss.
With naught a worry, nor a wonder in front of me
Nor the delicious irony of the creature I turned out to be.
And just as often, I have pondered the concept
That dwells within these tawdry emotions.
These bright tendrils of thought, but thought not.
All of these perils of existence, of feeling alive
Brings me back around in a circle once more
To that moment of my birth, those things that torture me.
I feel mountains of pain that flourish inside my soul
A flower of life with sprinkles of wants and goals.
All I want to do is suck the rage out of me and gambol.
I feel innocence that beckons with quiet refrain
A touch, a whisper, a hint of something unlike pain
I don't know what to do with this ill-gotten gain.
I am a walking ruin of pain and innocence
My tread upon this earth brings fear and mistrust
Fierce, monstrous emotions that cross my visage.
A twisted, wretched defiantly misshapen mien
I am a man made monster, a man made thing.
I am the monster put together by Doctor Frankenstein.

LIQUID SONGS

Beneath the surface calm, the trouble boils
Simmering anger, as the beasts slowly coil.
The surface world a despicable place in their eyes
Full of wanton practices and disgusting cries.
Best left alone, that world of pestilence and woe
Best to remain beneath the surface, far below.
Tenfold the sound is terribly wrong,
Like the notes from a forgotten song.
From the deeps there comes a warrior
Full of fight and lots of courageous vigor.
And yet, as with so many vices above the surface
The calm is broken by their sick, sick embrace.
The intrusions into the deep are unwanted
And yet still they arise, scare tactics undaunted.
More direct approaches would then be required
Before the world beneath the surface becomes mired.
Tenfold the sound is terribly sung
Like the steps from a forgotten rung.
From the deeps there comes such vigor
Full of fight, this courageous warrior.
Undeterred, the landlocked continue to interfere
With those that exist beneath the watery frontier.
The creature knows that Man has his own ways
Therefore he must take this fight to their mainstays.
From deep below the waves, surrounded by song
To the surface, where he must correct this wrong.
Tenfold the sound is terribly right
Like the notes from a forgotten fright.
From the deeps there comes a creature
Full of fight and lots of fearsome features.
Silent like thunder heard beneath the waves
He strikes out amongst the Human enclaves.
Terror, the weapon of choice he must use
In scaring the surface dwellers to choose:
To stay away and disrupt the waves below
Or face the wrath of creatures' fearsome blows.

UNDER WRAPS

Explain this gravity to me:
What matter of import?
What manner of transport?
How is it that this vessel
Has become so entombed?
Within this cage of stone
A lumbering resting place?
And who, with their mind
Set well in a skull living
Seeks to disturb this grave
With so much unforgiving?
This vessel, this body so old,
Forgotten by many told
A guardian to preserve
The body of a dead prince,
One so long past and buried
Past the time of the now
And forever wrapped
In trappings and bandages
Of a bygone, dusty Age
Of Majesty, awe and power.
We tremble in our shadows
As the guardian shuffles by
Seeking he who dared to enter
The tomb of just left of center
In the Valley of the Kings
There shall be scorpion stings
And the dusty remnants of
The Mummy's revenge.

THE STORY OF JOE #2

He's mad I say, mad; mad as a loon!
Have you seen what lurks below?
Below, down there, in his lab hidden?
It's a terrible secret, I must say.
Something so horrible,
It must be hidden, locked away.
I crept into his lab one day.
A frightened creature I was
Lurking amongst the vials
The beakers, the alembics,
The arcs of electric menace,
The scent of not quite right.
And surprised I was, by the sight:
Of all this chaotic mystery left about.
There was a flourish of chemicals
Fitful and fiery, as they clashed
Across tables overflowing with notes
And instruments of unknowable devices.
To my dismay, I spied him in the corner
His wicked grin plastered something thin
Across his pasty face, glistening at me.
I froze, startled by this grimace of madness
As sure, I was, to this day that he meant
Me harm in some wicked, wicked way.
I ran, as fast as I could to get away.
But, we must return to this den of evil
To cleanse the stain that lurks therein.
Won't you come with me now?
Please sir, you and I, I know
We can make a difference there.
We'll just sneak in quiet as can be.
Light a few chemicals and unleash
A torrent of destruction to finish
Him and his creations once and for all.
I'm sure we can do it, sir, you and I
Come, let's be off to save the day.

SQUISH

I am, he who is organic matter loosely collected
        into a wide-ranging heap of random clutter.
I am, he who is a fearsome creature of gluttony
        and the cacophony of ceaseless dementias.
I am, he who is forward fed by countless digestive
        acids which break down my prey of choice.
Anything living, is something to consume
There is no creature I'd prefer to exhume
Everything here, is the building of your tomb
I bide my time, as I await your gooey doom.
You are, the motley assortment of peoples
        randomly scattered across the land far.
You are, the sheep that dot the landscape with fear
        and rage and all the food that I desire
You are, the prey whose bones I shall suck clean
        of all organic material, bit by bloody bit.
No space is too small for me to fit in
You cannot hide, so don't even begin
To run away, especially with your skin.
There's no escape - you cannot hope to win.
We are, the dichotomy of feed and fed
        sometimes living, sometimes dead.
We are, the cycle of consumption and waste
        as we dance reckless about in our haste
We are, all that remains or will remain after
        all that disappears, especially laughter.
And after all is said and done
There's nothing else more fun
Than to chase my prey, I wish
And then everything just goes squish…

LADIES OF THE NIGHT

Who, who shall burn for me?
As I stand watching the gallows tree?
Cavorting 'round the Devil's Knee?
We bent ladies cackling merrily
Plucking and poking at thee.

Who, who shall burn with me?
As I spit upon the conventions mundane
The peasants and their trite refrains.
A call to the Devil made in exchange
For a sacrifice worthy of the gain.

Who, who shall burn without me?
As I fly away upon broomstick mine
Spinning havoc and cries and discord
My Craft carefully constructed with blood
Spilt upon the ground to my liege-lord.

Who, who shall burn the lives left behind?
Those souls that I have yet to feast upon?
Wicked are they, those left to rot
Wicked will they be as they roast below
Wicked I shall send them in but an eon away.

Who, who shall burn?
I say, why not everyone ....

BRIGHT LIGHTS, ALIEN SIGHTS

Twinkling little stars above
This night, so very bright
I wish only to see what I see
What other kinds of mystery.
Sharp and silvery dome
Flying fast, free to roam.
Upon jets of alien tech
All shiny and sparkly chrome.
Wonder we, what they want?
Is it a simple journey of curiosity?
Or something much more malign?
Maybe all they want are directions?
Now they've landed, and approach.
We gather as a flock to see and gawk.
Look at their oddness, how they dress.
It's a party, for sure, but I digress.
Motioned into their craft we gather
Like cattle, or sheep if you'd rather.
I don't know what it means either
And I don't like the look of that neither.
And what is it with this probe?
The one that has been placed
Up the backside, where never
Before, a probe has been put?
Speaks wonders, I'm sure to say
What they want, and who will pay?
This is a moment, here, now, today.
The Aliens are amongst us, no way!
I want to get off this crazy trip.
Never bargained for any of this;
Especially not with what I've heard.
They've got us trained to …

Ghost Dreams

Ghost dreams and insidious screams
From out behind the dresser drawer
He lurks and finds a hidden horror.

Behind that crazy wall or door
Cry out, cry out, his hand is near
Everywhere you have ever felt fear.

Death, no doubt his calling card.
By any other name, I'd call it foul
This twisted capering deadly howl.
One whisper, one shout is all you get;
The Boogey Man by another name
As he crafts his terror and his shame.
Ages past and stories long past forgot;
It's obvious that from underneath the bed
One might win, or one might lose one's head.
He's a monstrous piece of work, sure as sugar.
Just remember one more thing if nothing more:
Don't forget to look behind each and every door!

In The Deep Dark Woods

In the Deep Dark Woods, everybody cries
In the Deep Dark Woods, everybody dies
In the Deep Dark Woods, something's gonna happen,
In the Deep Dark Woods.

Have you heard of the tales, told of fell creatures that reside
In these dark woods of old and drear? Of shadows and fear?
Can you see their movements, so lithe, so quick, so unclear?
Just behind that shadow, hiding behind that leaf, a shape
One which crafts despair, pain and agony without effort
And just as easily disappears, once again a shadow, gone.

In the Deep Dark Woods, they own the shadows
In the Deep Dark Woods, they own the shallows
In the Deep Dark Woods, don't get caught in the open,
In the Deep Dark Woods.

Laughing, they are the masters that own these woods.
The soul of terrible curses and vengeance disturbed
Free to run foul, to run amok the debris of Nature.
Wild and unchecked, unfettered and chaotic indeed
These creatures are the essence of the deep dark woods
A guttural stench of death, a story that remains untold!

In the Deep Dark Woods, terror is inevitable
In the Deep Dark Woods, escape is impossible
In the Deep Dark Woods, slaughter is not just an option,
In the Deep Dark Woods.

Bill Snider

WING AND A PRAYER

Mean, unsightly and unclean
Things of the disgusting ways
A Devil in female form.
From the cradle filth torn.

Fear the beast with talon and claw
Their wicked shrilling caw caw caw
Enough to drive
One fully insane.

Fetid odours that waft and weave
Unpleasant violent harmonies
Talon and beak
Wreck and shriek.

Fearsome, twisted and unseen
Odiferous, insidious and obscene
From the sky they drop
Like fecal matter: plop, plop, plop.

Vicious creatures, full of spite
Capricious little catamites
Flock of Harpies taking flight
Hurling shit through this fight.

Lost in their battle song
They carry dark fear along
No end this obscene wrong
The stench doesn't belong!

From the tortured woods
Pain, their only made goods
And nothing ever should
Be as devilishly understood:

That a Harpies' way of life
Is something born of strife
Existing violently like a knife
I wouldn't want one as a wife!

I AM HARPY

Bitterness and pain, my wayward companions
This entire world crawling with life and disdain
Creatures of flesh and spirit and happenstance
Figments of godless hoarders and miscreants
Pity them their lacklustre life and ruins
Their playtimes filled with food and refrain.
My time upon this plain of existence is moot
Barefoot and airborne, I fly high above this land
Spying the
I am not happy,
I am Harpy.

ZOMBIES IN THE JUNGLE

There is a sound that permeates
The air rich in bass and moisture
Something menacing looming
Dense and drear, inducing fear.

Drums, thrumming, beating distant rhythms.
Chanting, blood flowing, distant nightmares.

Missing and presumed deceased
Buried and forgotten, life released.
Jungles absorb the living and dead
Foliage grows over the past, forgot.

Drums, thrumming, beating distant rhythms.
Blood boiling, the rhythm always changing.

Many things that crawl and fly and
Wander through the dense jungles
Things to fear, many things so near
But most of all, that which is unseen.

Drums, thrumming, beating distant rhythms.
Shifting, shaping, curled deep within, within.

The tempo of the drums, so distant heard
Rattle the bones of the earth, like thunder
Looming menace parts green underbrush
Releasing the captive held within its grasp.

Drums, thrumming, beating distant rhythms.
The safe world once held behind, long gone.

There it is, the creature, now from the depths
His eyes, dead and milky, his lips sewn shut
What does it want and who does it serve?
Wheresoever it goes, we don't not want to know.

Drums, thrumming, beating distant rhythms.
Stay away from the Voodoo, it's best that way...

Vengeance

My head, it seems to have been stolen again.
As I seek out those who had me put to the axe;
For it is by their hands, that I, this spectre roams
These ungodly lands, betwixt life and death dark
My home, headless though I be.

I did not commit the crime of which I was accused
Yet surely, did your ancestors strike me down for it.
This night is bright with promise, something I like;
The possibility of being reunited once again, whole.
My body, headless though it be.

It is vengeance that I seek, upon the skein of your life
You were not the one to wield the blade, but nonetheless
Descended you are from their progeny, and that I will strike.
To regain a measure of my honour, lost so very long ago.
My life, headless though it is.

To sleep forever more, upon the bones of the earth
Cleaved as I have been for so long to this misty land
Your life is forfeit, for only when they are all expunged
Will I regain my body, my home, my honour and my head.
My honour, headless though it is.

DOWN TO THE DUST

The word of God upon thy brow
You are alive, in the world now
Creature of Man, bereft of soul
You cannot fathom your role
From the mud and the dust
Your construct has been risen
Given form to perform tasks
By men of faith and masks
"Truth" you are christened
To the word of stated deed
You hearken and listened
Your duties lie amongst
Dark and smaller places
Down amongst the mud
Flecked with pain, blood
Your history, your future
Written cold, concrete
Down to the Dust
Where once the
Body of you
Once lay
You will
Return
Dust...

WICKED

Death, thou art a wicked black fiend
A taste of life and we're wiped clean.
Pulled from this shell
A broken kind of hell
Spun away this spell.

Spiritual bankruptcy, moral decay
The fibres of life left, cast astray
Denied a veritable curse
What makes it worse
Is that's another verse.

still you cast your lot within
Breaching life and collecting sin
No simple life for thee
A creature of calamity
Just another soul jerky.

Is that all that we are to you, sir?
Some form of collective blur?
Nothing other than one more?
Another tepid soul in a drawer?
Just a job for now, closing a door?

Cast not my head in shame
I've lived my life without blame.
You can have this dirty old shell
And the rest of it can go to hell.
There's nothing left, just a smell.

Death, thou art wicked, obscene
A veritable chorus of vicious means.
Grim Reaper that you are
Characterization bizarre
Not quite the shiniest star.

But then, that's just what you are ...

ESSENCE

Essence of man, the soul of pain
Weary, tired, attached to this coil;
In depth of journey, a lifetime spent
Pursuing the dream of life, life of a dream.
Suck, suck Succubae
Suck this guy, suck him dry.
Suck, suck Succubus
Kill, kill, kill for us.
A hunger without satiation or bliss
Marked by wicked embrace, the kiss.
Creatures that roil through the ether
Searching for victims to tether.
Suck, suck Succubae
Suck his soul, suck him dry.
Suck, suck Succubus
Die, die, die for us.
Invisible threads that attach to prey
Hope without hope that they'll go away.
A moment's pleasure spent on the lips
Carried away by will o' the wisps.
Suck, suck Succubae
Suck his life, suck this guy.
Suck, suck Succubus
Feed, feed, feed for us.
Empty shells are all that remain
Hopeless victims left to rot, again.
Bounteous beauty free to roam
Draining the essence of anyone's home.
Suck, suck Succubae
Drain him till he dies.
Suck, suck Succubus
Little mess, little fuss.

MADNESS

BITTEN

A blank screen.
A fate left unwritten.
A hand turned against Beast and Man.
A life once bitten.

All elements of being congeal into the makeup of life.
Our moments of glory, our thoughts of happiness, joy;
The different things that make us the individuals that we are.
Separately, we are microcosmic phlegm on the Earth.
Scratching our existence raw from the soil we tread upon.
Each turn of a leaf, each jab into the wound into the ground.
And still we stand. Collectively, as a bunch of individuals,
Never as a commonly united species of understanding.

Many gifts we number that we spill upon this land we inhabit.
Laughter, song, dance, thoughts of Brightness connected.
Children scattering throughout a township's commons
The blessings of many people united by their kinship
A closeness to life, a freedom to wonder about existence
Both mundane and sublime; a feature of contemplation.

Many dooms we birth from out of barren souls, wretchedness.
Hatred, fear, disease, weapons of destruction and ill purpose.
Black hands of shadow puppets silently stalking across life
Infecting the living with misdeeds and caustic toxicity
A death that creeps with the face of innocence blackened
Both fearsome and hungry; a regret of sophistication.

The weight of being human, and alive, and during this time.
It fills with both wonder and disdain, at how much good and
    bad
Is wrought by our hands, those that we call our brethren and
    kin.
The end will arrive in its appointed hour, we all will be there
    then

25

And truly the only measurement worth caring for at that
        moment
Is whether or not, as an individual, were we true to ourselves?
Or whether we allowed ourselves to willfully forget our
        connections?
In the end, we are what we are; but there is more that we could
        be.

An indelible example.
An altruistic experiment.
An existence full of Nature and Man.
An opportunity to excel.

DIEHARD DECADENCE

Diehard decadence, perpetual motion machine
One hand clapped, and all became obscene!
This odiferous lifestyle, perfidy entrenched
Cookies without milk, how can they be drenched?
I want to be a hippy, but the machine won't let me
It's calculated the odds, which made me a zombie.
The monster inside, eats away at the crust of I
And those around who lurk slowly, vilely die.
I know it's not a merry tune I sing this day,
But life is funny in this and many other ways.
I sing the light, darkly and spry, soft and cracked
But ultimately I come to the party partially whacked!
There is no end in sight, there is only more of this Bright
Come with me, this evening and every other night!
Join my movement, join my adventure, join my Team
We've got cookies that will absolutely make you SCREAM!

Bill Snider

Is This A Cookie...?

Is this a cookie which I see before me,
The crumble toward my hand? Come, let me taste thee.
I have thee not, and yet I taste thee still.
Art thou not, scrumptious vision, sensible
To feeling as to taste? or art thou but
A cookie of the mind, a false obsession,
Proceeding from the heat-consumed brain?
I see thee yet, in form as sensuous
As this which now I feed.
Thou deliver'st me the way that I was feeding;
And such a consumptive I was to use.
Mine buds are made the fools o' the other senses,
Or else worth all the rest; I taste thee still,
And on thy plate and dudgeon gouts of chips,
Which was not so before. There's no such thing:
It is the bloody chocolate which informs
Thus to mine eyes. Now o'er the one halfworld
Nature seems dead, and wicked dreams abuse
The curtain'd sleep; witchcraft celebrates
Pale Hecate's offerings, and wither'd murder,
Alarum'd by his sentinel, the wolf,
Whose howl's his watch, thus with his stealthy pace.
With Tarquin's ravishing strides, towards his design
Moves like a ghost. Thou sure and firm-set earth,
Hear not my steps, which way they walk, for fear
Thy very stones prate of my whereabout,
And take the present horror from the time,
Which now suits with it. Whiles I threat, he lives:
Words to the heat of deeds too cold breath gives:
Cookie!

HIDE LITTLE SISTER

Hide little sister, hide in the dark
Hide little sister, hide from the dead

We know where you hid the cookies, we know where the body's
       been bled.
Your reign of villainy ends this night, full of shadows, full of
       fruition sped.
Is it the body or is it the mind, that remembers the song, that
       remembers the dream?
Does the pattern of the dance remain the same or does it change
       from season to scream?

Hide little sister, hide in the dark
Hide little sister, hide from the dead

The sun rises in the sky, the moon flies away with sad cow eyes;
The spiders skitter about looking for clues amongst the rafters of
       a soul
Seeded with chaos and shadows that rust, endlessly tiring in the
       pursuit
                    of redemption and a chance at cornucopia ...

Hide little sister, hide in the dark
Hide little sister, hide from the dead

At the centre of silence, we sing our song, our song of grace.
There are no more of the shadows, the sweet, the hidden,
The little twisted spiders that crawled across the spines of
       insanity,
Lost, unresolved, spiraling out of control, out of time and space.

Hide little sister, hide in the dark
Hide little sister, hide from the dead

No matter what you do, no matter where you run
We'll be there, waiting, once this game has begun.
It's a dance, one made for you, tailored, and spun
The play's the thing, now that everything's been done.

Hide little sister, hide in the dark
Hide little sister, hide from the dead

For we always come back, just for one more kick at the can …
Voices of silence, an army of life set against a backdrop of night;
evil thy word, thy sword, thy wicked way of violence and silence;
against the backdrop of bright … seek, a voice, in the wind, the
willow that follows no song, but its own … find the centre and
lick it - 'cause it's the scary secret …

ALL YOUR BASES ARE BELONG TO US

When it slithers forward, it is said to be born anew.
When it follows format, it is said to be one with that which
        preceded the now.
When it fears neither now or then, it is said to be one of them.
When it features zombie chickens, it is said to be rather
        whacked.
When it swallows the souls of the unrepentant, it is said to be
        satiated.

I am come, the master of evil.
I am spared, the mercy of the unforgiven.
I am delimited, by ASCII not RTF.
I am structured, but by no means not random.
And thus I am, but what will I become?

It is upon this night, no doubt
That change shall be wrought
Fair, foul, funky, fowl
This night, anon, the twist
Shall be weaved into the vein.
Fear not, fear not
For this Zombie's hot!

Ready or not, the time has been struck
From the highest peak, the furthest track of land
Now and forever more, the silence has been born
And the world shall tremble anew by the means left askew.
Time sits still, at the peak of its spark
Ligatures of being spun round the fire stack
Imperious legions trampled by the storm
Down, deep in the dark place of histories past
Something new shall arise, something spun.

Into the Pitt, you vile dark thing!
Into the Pitt, with teeth and claw!
Into the Pitt, seek and find resource!
Into the Pitt, good Librarians! Into the Pitt!

Dreams live in accord to the time and spirit invested into them.
Luck plays a part, but only plays second fiddle to hard work.
Time and tide stay the hand of no mane such as those that hope.
And in the doing, by being, by living in hope, shall survive past
        the dawn.

What means the form from which we arrive?
By hook or by crook, or by fiddle faddle attrition?
Whereupon the crime of life is excised by volition?
Cease the attempt, and all is lost, foresworn.
What's in a name? Nothing but a game.
What's in a title? Nothing by recital.
What's in a theory? Nothing but dreary.
What's that outside? Oh, that's nothing dear.

Hear me Zombie--hear me roar.
There's nothing outside your door.
One Lone Zombie stands and delivers
Nothing but this one wordy word more.

Remember, if nothing else be true:
All Your Bases Are Belong To Us!

And that fellow "spirals of DNA species mammal groups",
"random contingents of wacky hullaballo" and "merry makers
of misidentified mayhem" would represent my pinnacle post. I
wonder what will happen now? What will become of the universe
now? Oh, my!
        Knock, knock.

CHICKENS OF DOOM

The birds have fallen from the trees;
The whistle bent upon fallen knee.
Truth, an elusive and reluctant hero
Ground into dust by all and zero.
A complex walk twixt dark and light
Simpering with rage against the night.
One more moment spent in context
Here, bide a time, until ready next.
Birth, again, at the feet of a maiden
Splayed upon a pattern I'd trade in.
And the broken cycle begins anon
One more twist, and then I'm gone.

Piece
Post
Predict

DOOM DOOM the chickens of doom are beginning to assemble.
Rejoice the cascade legions as the living are all a tremble.
Our jaunty little war song filled with clucks and punches
The meat and matter fill our belly with yummy lunches.
One quick cut and the artery is severed, neat, so clean
Death spills out, spinning, spinning, singing out it's dream.
A tick tock time explosion of fury and fowl movement
Ashen faces of expired avian callous bewilderment
Wanton destruction of all and sundry blister the land.
I assume the living will want to make a final stand.
Hearken, hear me thunder, hear me roar:
There's no way out of this one, dear;
Not even through the back door.

THE CAVE

The cave it waits but just ahead.
Air so thick and full of dread.
Moist like breath foul and clammy
Issues forth from darkness quiet.
Within those confines, something lurks.
Beady eyes with malice full
Gaze back at me upon the lip of temptation.

So quiet I stand as I gaze in deep.
Probing for clues as to what might be.
Decant the night, the cloying brightness
Bequeathed with pain, the lustre of life
And all about, the creatures of night stir.
Forlorn, bereft of hope I gather courage
Into the darkness befouled, I must trek.

Logic is a bomb that goes off in the head
Logic is a scary thing best left undead
Logic is a poem twisting out instead
Logic is rage tamed down until it's red.
Instinct is a beast worldly and wary
Instinct is a colourful hegemony
Instinct is a song of bright and dark
Instinct is a dance of death and life.

Something waits in the farther deeps.
The cave looks back at me, as I weep.
I can't go back, my fate pushes me in.
Without challenges, my life is a sin.
Sour the taste my sweat I swallow
As I walk, much like to the gallows.
And a moment burst, bright and clear.

Logic is a bomb colours everything else
Logic is a scary thing denied its best.
Logic is a poem wrangled to the ground.
Logic is rage broken, littered with sound.
Instinct is a beast of happenstance.
Instinct is a colourful party dance.
Instinct is a song full of can and can'ts.
Instinct is a dance with delicate balance.

I know that it lurks there, a monster, I'm sure.
Just waiting to rip me to shreds for dinner.
With any luck, my death will be quick, painless.
But my luck usually runs the other way, so ...
That's where I am and that's where I go.

Bill Snider

DARK PLACES

I'm in a dark place this evening.
A twisted, terrible corridor of misery.
There are horrible creatures that prowl
The byways of misbegotten events;
And I have become a statistic of one.
This moment has escaped my grasp
Spiraling away from me and my vision.
No more will I see that beautiful smile
Of my girlfriend as she danced, or sung
Lightly, brightly that evening's joyous cant.

Piss, pain, fecal matter, blood all round.
This is life, this is raw, this is how it ends.

Blood, it is all around me, staining my clothes.
Is it mine, is it hers, is it torn from someone else?
There is so much blood, pouring over my hands.
It covers the walls, it covers the floors, it's all over
Everything, cloying, clotting, sinking rotting deep
Across everything that was beautiful, everything bright.
The light has escaped her eyes, her doorways true
Never again, will I see them sparkle, nor dance
Nor cascade across a nighttime embrace.

Blood, piss, fecal matter, pain all round.
This is death, this is messy, this it where it darkens.

Pain, raw and searing, clamouring against my ribs
Seeking escape, seeking freedom, seeking targets.
Random splatter of dichotomies and disorderly conduct.
The night breathes and there is nothing wrong with me.
I can feel it, I can hear it, I know it - this is the right way.
Tastes are filling the air and I can but reach them
With hunger comes the manner of clean dispatch
And the best method in which to feed from life.
I come kicking, clawing, freed from remorse.

Fecal matter, blood, pain, piss all round.
This is real, this is the now, this is how it grows.

Pissing against the wind, the historic flight of life.
I am not the animal I once was, this beast of mud.
There is something new stirring in my blood, cold.
The love of my life is nothing more here on the ground
But a discarded husk from which I've sucked the life
Bloody and complete, formless and discrete.
Esoteric schematics of nether regions unfathomable
Open before my eyes as I gaze rapt in dismay
At the plan spread before my life, species and decayed.

Pain, blood, piss, fecal matter all round.
This is birth, this is creation, this is where it starts.

Shit! This is where it begins to hit the fan and scatters.
I never knew what kind of could possibly shift this way
But there it is, deep, dark and decayed past capacity.
There is evil here, and my choices are less clear now.
Gifts have been bestowed, upon myself unclear,
And many others who wield them less charitably.
There are creatures that move with care in the night.
This now is my lot in life, one that I must make count.
I am a creature born of blood, piss, pain and shit.

Piss, pain, shit, blood, and war all round.
This is war, this is conflict, this is how it's done.

And with these gifts I am something gross, something other
Reborn neither by machine nor human, caring mother.
This dark place from which I now have become born
At the expense of my girlfriend, her life cruelly torn.
I will not stop, I will not rest, I will not lay down and plead
Against this depravity that has wrest from me my deeds.
The creatures that created this situation I will hunt to the end
Their lives, their fortunes, whether they be enemy or friend.
War, it will have many casualties, but this will not stop me
As I take my vengeance across time, space and all reality!

TRICK OR TREAT

Trick or treat, tasty feet
Where oh where are my
Yummy things to eat?

Trick or feat, nasty sheet
How come you continue
To hoard what I want to eat?

Trick or sweet, evil meat
Look at all the children
Roaming through the street.

Trick or pleat, where's my fleet
Of Zombie minions shuffling
Hither, thither and discrete?

Tricky beats, in their seats
Deadly creatures of darkness
Making the apocalypse complete

Trick or greet, deadly elite
Friendly denizens of the dark;
I think I'll end by consuming Pete.

I want candy ...
I want cookies ...
I want brains ...
I want bacon ...
Can you give me
Something full
Of all the stuff
That's bad for me?

THERE ARE DREAMS TRAPPED BENEATH MY FINGERNAILS

There are dreams trapped beneath my fingernails. They're not my dreams, no; but rather those of others whose dreams have become trapped there, whilst I rip their craniums free of their former use. What need has one for a dream, when one's brain has been ripped apart and eaten by a zombie? And yet, those dreams are still trapped beneath my fingernails...

The dreams have begun to scream once again. They tap, tap, tap on the melon I wear for a head. But alas, they just won't stay completely dead. I turned to ask the ravens who live outside my window, what their thought was on my plight. They just looked askance at me and said good night. The dreams have driven all thoughts out of my brain.

My dreams are bleeding, this night. I ask the ravens again, and something just ain't right. They laugh at me, raucously, derisively. They point and shoo, and look at me as if I've stepped in pooh. How does one compete with that? Again, a little bit of blood seeps out from this dream, and knocks me about just that little bit more ...

The angels are crying, as the blood is drying. There are no dreams left for me to cry, and the only words from the ravens are "die, die die." The spider webs from behind my eyes, have crusted over and begun to lie. I know they talk to the ravens, and yet still they deny. I shall be avenged for this perfidy, verily though I walk the shadows of doom ....

SPIDDLEYDINK

Spiddleydinkie dinkie doo.
Spiddleydink, Spiddleydink
Spiddleydinkify the whack a doo.

Spiddleydinkie dinkie doo.
What for, where art thou
Thou Spiddleydinkie doo?

If not for the shade,
This side of roast beef
Spiddleydink, I see you.

Spiddleydinkie dinkie doo
I'm quite fine, Spiddleydink
I don't know, how about you?

BITS

Bring on the guts, the gore, the gleeful abandon of dichotomy!
Steal the gates closed and blast past the careless disregard.
Spires and rundels and drawbridges abound the moors
Shrieks that howl through the darkest and cruel of lures.
I speak not of the monster that lurks within
But rather the humans that constantly spin.
Forever aimless upon the dance floor
Here we have another, just one more.

Insane I am, return I have to the gyre.
Fire I am in need of, for what I aspire.
The reed, the pipe, the broken spire!
Spiral architects breaking all the rules
And the whole is swallowed up by ghouls.
Let us not be taken by them silly fools.

Random Fu me this.
Random Fu me that.
Who's afraid of a ...
... zombie flying bat?

Topic?
Tropic.
Stay by the saw pic.
If I had the right trick
I'd be able to think thick.
There are no tables here
And now I must run dear
Right through the door
And out into more gore.
Laughter, light and little things
That crisp and crackle strings.
A final resounding last clasp
As the crowd reaches past
The comfort zone knowing
That life is just another bow ring.

Reach for the prize
It lies just inside
The soul of a child
The star of a monster
Fickle as the hand of Fate
And tricksey just like Hobbits'
Bequeathed upon the rabbits' warren
A quest, a grail, a frail signature barren.
Peach fuzz and raspberry ginger ale
All that brings down to the little grail
One last moment, one last blast
To trumpet the end, to begin again.
Peace, marked by the wind of gone
Twixt this space and that time
A-righted within the page of nine
And twisted by the souls of mine
I stand and gaze once more
At the edge of sanity's grace
And wonder again
Why so serious?

Chaos lives inside me.
It feeds, it lives, it twists.
Each moment ticks by
And never will it die.

Chaos is my neighbour
I live with its constant natter
It tries its best all the time
To make my head go splatter.

Chaos is a beast I dance with
No matter where I end up
The beast is always closer
Than the last breath I've taken.

Blood

Blood and boil
Trouble and toil
Twisted bit of finger
And a little more that lingers
Find the hollow spot in life
And dig it out, with fire
With burrowing spite
With devil's light
Watch, worry
The End
Is nigh

I am getting old; I am getting decrepit.
Am I gaining wisdom, am I gaining knowledge?
Or am I gaining buckets of nothing but woe?

Blood, it spills, it spoils, it finds
A path twixt now and then
And comes but once again.

Twilight darkness finds me here this moment
Wondering why there is no light in this place
Something more that must be beyond this pale.

Blood, it spills, it spoils, it finds
A path twixt now and then
And comes but once again.

Wellsprings of terror bubble from beneath my feet.
It echoes with the talents that I fear I have not
And hatches the monster of doubt, of loss.

Blood, it spills, it spoils, it finds
A path twixt now and then
And comes but once again.

Hollow witlessness is my only champion now
My only friend, true still this moment forward
Even as the dawn still tries to claw it's way up.

Blood, it spills, it spoils, it finds
A path twixt now and then
And comes but once again.

With the days light amongst us once more
The charade of commonality is again our feast.
Let us feed and forget the past, as it is done.

Blood, it spills, it spoils, it finds
A path twixt now and then
And comes but once again.

RIDDLES

Cloaked in riddle
Hidden in rhyme
History, fortunes
Lurking in time.

Smoke and mirrors
Snakes and sonnets
Life, paid in full
Trapped in secrets.

Fury wrested free of
The mediocre deviltry
Tapered string theory
Wrapped in poetry.

Time tick, evil intent
The clock spins in time
Meter, the future spent
Villains stuck in crime.

Burned alive by simple fear
Buried by hatred's broken spear
Imperfect journey under the sun
The end is almost near.

Moments, frozen and gone
Tempered by hazard's edge
Broken, discarded and bled
Fragments left of the bone.

Wonder ceases glory lost
Time tick, winding down
Riddle thought buried
Graveyard ghost fallen.

Carved in headstone
The words of passing
Bless this fallen one
No rest, those who sing.

One last line to be said
A passing that is sped.
In this rhyme is bled
Time is dead.

My Weird

Terror spills from my side, as I sit here in the dark. I look out of
this shell, and wonder: Why do the little monsters all
run away?

Don't they want to come out and play? A game of sticks? A swig
of a happy moment to dance and sing and cavort the
way one used to do?

Or is it a measure of the day, of the times we harken back upon
older thoughts, of graveyard stillness and deathly
droughts?

Sad. I am to see this smallish story bleeding out through its
pages. And I weep, for tis unfinished, this tale, this
mirror of agony.

Must I thus strike up the Devil and rouse it anew? Must I poke it
and make it spew? Must I Shout at this Devil with
mighty voice?

Or is it true what they say: The End is Nigh. And zombies are
soon to roam ....

Hell has spoken to me this day, the final one upon which you
living souls continue to believe is still safe and natural.

It spoke of many things, both grim and dire. Of blasted flowers
and wilted spirits lost in darkness and decay.

And too, it spoke, of the plans to remake the world, shaped
anew in an image born of pain, anguish, misery and
dismay.

A truly zombie kind of game, this tawdry little tale. Wefts and
weaves of living and dead and all the things that bump
in the night.

This weave upon which I light my candle this night, leaves me
in an unusual place, of darkness and light mixed.

In the tepid pool of soul sucking disbelief, the sour of the long
dark crawls over my light heartedness.

Impaled upon my brightness, my dark lashes out with fear. The
price, this weird, my soul, my body, my zombie
likeness.

Leashed, lashed, lacquered for an Eternity of being, an Infinity of
thought, deep within the bowels of I that is I.

There lurks both monster and poet, mayhem and merriment, life
and death, being and being not.

All, one big melting pot of self. Wrapped into and about, my
weird, my life, my I that is I.

My Weird, Part 2

My Weird wants to get out.
But I'm keeping it locked up.
It's probably for the best
If I keep it close to my chest.

I feel that I might burst
With this energy cursed
A moment is all it takes
For this little writer to flake.

Just one twinkle from a star
No matter how close, how far.
Energy courses throughout all
As my Weird takes me past the fall.

And now my journey whispers thin
While monsters crawl under my skin.
Sick I feel, that it might never stop now
When the creeping Weird breaks my vow.

There are things that speak of dread and wonder
All of them come from lands both above and under.
I query the feelings tapping within my skull for a clue
The intangibles of life both exquisite and stuck like glue.

The mists of time escape my vision, as everything dims
Oh so quietly, the voice, the vision moves back within.
Waif thin and just as delicately honed this pack
Wailing in grief, in joy: Back, back, Back!

As they clamour, I crawl back inside
The temple of my soul that's cried
Close to the birth of living
As with this, this giving.

My Weird is calling again, it wants to play.
This time I think I'll try it out at least once
To see what might be seen, for the nonce.
Emptiness beckons, filled with bright decay.

In the distance, I hear a sound, my name.
Something to do about a vicious little game.
Life, they called it, something fulfilling they said.
It's better off, better anyways than being dead.

The din in the background is filled with a raucous noise.
My Weird is out back playing with its wicked little toys;
Wit, whisper, wonder, and mayhem the best of the bunch.
Quietly they gather, deciding what's best today for lunch.

I'm stuck. Between the right and wrong and maybe of it all.
Is the Weird just screwing with me in order to get a head?
Or is it just sowing seeds of discontent in order have a ball?
Could it be something positive that seeks move me forward?

But my Weird keeps sending me these odd messages.
Neither text, nor Twitter, nor messenger pigeon comes.
Merely a thought, a whim, and out come some crumbs.
A glint, a glimpse, a tasty morsel of something more beyond.

A twist, by fate, both fickle and foul, this tidbit trickles out.
We have an oath, an honor to maintain, for this course.
Be Weird, by happy, be oneself if naught else this day
And everything else will work out as it should no doubt.

MY WEIRD, PART 3

My weird is playing with my faculties once again.
It calls out, it hollers with voice made hoarse
And a dimness of being fills the empty places.
This tired cacophony of terror and verve
Constantly at war with every little last nerve.
Spread out and cast down upon the canyons
Of hope, of joy, of misery, of disdain and more.
Spiritual growth betrayed by a sorrow grown dark
By the pyres spaced close and densely packed.

My weird is calling out to the farther reaches of space.
What it seeks, I cannot name, nor put a thought out of place.
Distant, distant planes of misshapen discords ring out
Against the black-drop of immensity and night.
My screams against this alternative direction
Go unheeded, unbidden, the anger sparks, directionless.
And each drop of my pain fills the void that much more.
Hearken, what is that, I ken? Is it an answer to my voice?
Or, more like, is it the doom that waits and preys on despair?

My weird has found an answer, within the belly of this beast.
My feet, or so it seems to me, has become a delectable feast.
Tendrils from some unholy spot deep outside of the universe
Crawl into the place I once housed my soul, my brain, my me.
Icy hot, the ravages of an age of pain and dark desires
Scours clean the husk of this vessel, in preparation, in wait.
I know it lurks there, behind my eyes, just waiting for that
        moment;
A time, a thought, an errant, erratic thought splotch to set it
        loose.
Something must be done to stop this infamy, but what?

My weird has gone to sleep, thoughtfully leaving me alone
With the perceptions heightened thus, a thing carrying within.
I suppose it is amused with me, and my attempts to be rid of it
But I cannot stop trying to be, that which I know that I am.
I am a slayer of dragons, an emulsifier of dangerous demons.

No manner of weird can ride me greater than the weird that I
    am.
But my time, I must bide, while this demon beast within me
    rides.
Solutions will be found, never fear, never abandon that hope.
As I slog it out still, with all that baggage that cries behind my
    eyes.

My weird, I know it continues to laugh at me and what I've
    done.
Stripped this demon beast, from me, I have managed to do.
What oh what, you say, can it possibly gain me to bare my soul
    thus?
And within what context the cost it should weigh on what
    remains?
To that I must say, the cost it is what it is, and must be paid
While this monstrous villainy continues to be over played.
Now, this morn, so bright, so baleful, sits in front of me again.
And I cast my gaze forward, deep into the icy, ink black dark
While I wait for the beast to return, to try once again.

My Weird, Part 4

Something is scratching, behind my left ear.
I cannot describe, though it is quite clear.
There's a rustling sort of feel to it, creepy.
In moments, I'm sure, I'll be too sleepy.
To wrest from it a meaningful scream
And a fall from grace, slipping to a dream.
The weird is restless this evening dark
Playing with fire, hoping to drive a spark.
A pretty little word or two it coughs out
A moment or three and then it will shout.
"Out, out, out damn voice of doom
I want you out of my head, my room."
My weird cares not, for my prattle, no.
To wherever it wants, that is where it will go.
And now, I grant unto thee, a moment of light
As the weird little voice inside, cackles in spite.
Cock up the morning, bring low the mizzen mast.
Something horrible, something from the past
Is going to be born on this awful, dead night.
Shiver, my bones, my soul, my undead sight.
There is evil afoot in the morning's gloaming
Something violent with wicked teeth foaming.
I cannot hide from this truth as I've seen
And still, I try to wake, from this wicked dream....

HUMANITY

The crazy voices in my head called me today. They asked me how things were going, and I told them, "Every-thing's peachy, 'cause that's how I am, and stuff." Then, I asked them how things were with them, and they told me.

They told me a tale of the beginning, of middles and endings.

They told me of the many things that exist throughout the world; of the beauty of falling leaves, and the horror of burning in stone. They told me about how a fish could live its entire life completely oblivious to the tedium by which its journey progresses along a predetermined path of circumstance and eventful highlights.

And they told me about the fear of knowing the complete set of details of a human existence when all of the moves have been planned out and are known, and all the moves have been seen, and repeated again and again.

They told me more things about how the plants that encompass the globe are interconnected by a complex chain of esoteric mystical energies that sustain each and every living thing in an enormity of bigness that could move a mountain to shed a tear at the shear brilliance of all those interdependent pinprick jots of congruity at the microcosmic level.

And they told me of the darkness that splits a hair and is cast out into the net of wonder, joy; about the network of terror that infiltrates and disrupts and disturbs and desecrates each and every relationship that imbues all of existence with the very energy with which it is created from.

They told me all of their crazy observations about life and about death and about the thousand and one other levels of being that may or may not be of relevance to the conscious mind. They repeated their didactic decrees until I was blue in the face. And then they repeated them again.

I heard what they had to say. I really did. And then they repeated it again. And again. And again. They filled me with their words that meant nothing, but spoke volumes of meaning about everythingness. The words they ensconced an eternity of existence wrapped up within a cookie of absolute discernment. And then they repeated it again.

I don't know what they want, what they wanted.

I do know, that they stopped their continuous repetition of what is, what was, what will be. And I do know a thing or two more now. For example, I know that the world is a really big place, and we are but a simple organism crawling upon its face. Granted, we move at a pace more in tune with the falling water from the mountaintop than we do the grace of the snail across the ground. But we are still a species that is not even close to achieving its potential. The snail moves at a snail's pace, as it has achieved the completeness for which the snail has achieved. No faster, no slower than the pace by which it has achieved, the snail's pace.

Humans, those of us still able to call themselves as such, what pace have we achieved? What, to what, have we become? Are we yet at the point to which we can point to our humanity and state that we have become the penultimate human that we can become? Or are we still on that path to attainment of such humanity?

Buried deep in our collective conscious unconsciousness, there lurks the beasts to which we cannot yet name. When we can name them, put paid service to the designs by which their existence owns up to our own place in the totality of everythingness, then perhaps we can say that we've arrived at the point to which our humanity is indeed the part to which we've arrived at. Perhaps not; yet still, we try.

And another thing that I know, is that the crazy voices in my head are not but a shadow of I, myself and only I; but instead, they are a reflection of the sum of all beings, both human and other, that permeate this realm of being. I don't know how or why or when or even wherefore art they? But they come, they say and they know what's what with what.

With infinite sadness and a stillness born of uncomfortable awareness and of blindness, we continue on our journey, faults and all, towards the completion of our existence, be it as a single cell amongst the machine, or the machine as a polyglot of all. With silence, with contemplation, with the desire to accomplish what we all know is attainable within ourselves, even at the smallest of combustible points, we can attain personal fulfillment without sacrificing, our humanity.

The last words that they spoke unto me, with quivering anticipation, I beheld their forms:

Vengeance fills the void.
Vengeance fills the mind.
Vengeance fills the ether between being and not quite so much.
When there is no more vengeance, then the journey begins in earnest.

And of that, of no more, do I know what they spake; for to delve even deeper into that maelstrom of being, would be to invite madness, and or worse.

Silence, it sits upon the open face of decision. You know it is right, when it is right, and you go forward with what it is. Speak now, this moment, and every one that follows that requires the word to be spoken, and make the silence count for what it counts for. Choose to be the moment; don't merely allow the moment dive into you and consume you, for you will be lost. Be, what you are, be what you will be, be Brightness. And be good with that.

Chaos, is the silence that has yet to speak. It is the right hand of getting things done, and the left hand of the things that have already done. It is the voice by which we attain our heights, and the slap in the face of flatulence by which we fail to even try. Speak it out, spell it with vigor, and choose to be what you can be.

And know, that above all else, cookies are still the best stuff on earth!

Have a nice Apocalypse!

DEAD SPACES

I hold my head up high
Even though everything around me
Is mostly, waiting to die.

Hope alone sleeps,
While all the King's men have perished;
Even the Queen weeps

Souls that I've taken
Buried so long ago in earthen graves
Have begun to waken.

Twisted, ugly beasts
Brooding malice darkens the lands
The dead and their feasts

Eyes that violated life
Searing past the vagaries and signs
Like a bloody knife.

Rage and thunder
Spiriting past the living and the dead
Tearing all asunder.

This is a mockery of being
One is inclined to scream out loud
And still everyone is fleeing.

The doom walks upright
Sprouting destruction and death
To everything in sight.

The days are grimmer
The nights are losing their lustre
The living grow dimmer.

Few remain alive, I know
Their lonely heartbeats but flutter
Spilt upon the dirty snow.

Is this the end, then?
Alone, amongst the darkness and death
Waiting my time, when?

The heavy, mutilated tread
Is only a few moments behind my space
It's the voices of the dead.

I run, I run, I run as if forever
Mired in a soupy miasma of dense, ichor;
And here, I thought I was clever

I waken from slumber
Tired, restless aware of the deeds
Performed in number.

This is another day I see
Not the nightmare that I witnessed;
But something I decree.

It was a black dream
Full of misery and despair and woe
Many souls did scream.

Going about my daily things
The mundane gluttony of civilization
Like a puppet with strings.

Wash, shave, clothe myself
Off to work and the drudgery therein
My life, put on its blue shelf.

On the path to work I stop
To stare at this fellow approaching me,
My bags forgot, they drop.

It's his eyes, you see
They're staring straight into my soul
Staring deep into me.

He's the one I saw in my dream
The destructive god of violence and death
I run and I want to scream!

MAYHEM

BUTTERFLIES

There's a store that I sometimes tapped on, rapping lightly, burning brightly, pointing at all the pretty butterflies that fluttered and scattered to the Heavens and sometimes returned.

I had more, but the butterflies ate them.

If I feed your paranoia, will you play with my dementia?
If I kick your hierarchy, will you slay my democracy?
If I slap your sadism, will you spin my puritanism?

It spins me 'round, like a jelly top, it spins my head so.
It sends me running, like angry bees, to and fro.
It reminds me of the life once lived so long ago.

But the butterflies ate all of my caramel corn.

And I can never go back to that store, ever again. As the insectoid creatures that birthed such beauty, have morphed into something worse, and the whole damn place needs to burn ....

Memories, they come, they go, but the after effects of their terror always remain, ingrained, in the wood, the air, the very space right there.

And sometimes, they burn ...

OF GOD AND MAN

The closer we come to God, the farther we get from Man.

Wherefore the sup of sensual lives spent in the glory?
What happenstance occurrence that blends our meanings?
Upon what skein is writ the pearls of wisdom and song?

The more we seek the solution of life, the farther we live from
home.

How fast, how far, how much, how now can you not fall?
What time is it, where are we now, are we there yet?
Can the end not be but a short stop amongst the trees?

When we set ourselves firmly aground, we become planted in
the ground.

And, in every corner of meaning, do we not see the shadows?
From the heights of lesser times, can we save ourselves from
folly?
Twixt the one and the other, does one or the other merit more?

In a time of endings, the beginnings end and begin again.

Time without measure, space without meaning
Twisted sketches of a future without colours
A collage of meaningless snippets of life
Bruised and braided together to form
A moderate burden of existence.
From my hand I cast a seed,
A germ of a simple idea.
A moment unstrung.
A thing of the past.

Wonders.

Screaming past the dark
An abyss full of pain and fury and rage
Lashing out against a world, a cosmos of cold certainty.
Steam-bound pent-up frustration fractured beyond repair or
sanity.

Flowering bright and diverse the chaotic freedom of living and
        dying
Peace and all of it's prospects painted fresh from the dichotomy
        of just be.
The midnight ride, all dark and dangerous follows the line of joy
        and fear.
Hearken, the journey calls to us, not so much the path that has
        been trod
As it is to the damnation of the final place of resting, deep in the
        past.
It is of God, of Man that the end is just as much one if not the
        other.
A path, a journey, a sordid tale spun in song and timbre.
One need but remember the times most past
To be sorrowed, to be succoured, to be
And then there is to all of that
The end is truly nigh.
Time once more ...

THE WORK IS FINISHED FOR THE DAY

The work is finished for the day,
        the time ticks quietly away.
I stand and share this thought,
        for the moment in time that it's caught:
Life without passion is a moment dried to sand.
Life without purpose is a clue that scatters from one's hand.
Life without meaning, is a dictionary without words
Meaning is elusive without context conclusive
Purpose is merry daft, floating by on a wooden raft
Passion is the devil's plaything, as we sit around spitting.

Now it is time to start something else,
        possibly something to convulse.
I sit and ruminate upon these moments,
        and hope that purpose is innocent.
Death without definition is a moment splattered.
Death without measure is a word uttered in despair.
Death without comfort is a castoff takeaway.
Definition is perplexing, in what manner most vexing.
Measure is despair, in a moment that doesn't care
Comfort is fleeting, in the ways that we are meeting.

... Time's up; I need a cookie.

Something

Answers to questions two.
In form of riddle just for you.
The answer to the first is yes
The answer to the next is yes.
Beyond that, anymore hullabaloo
And somebody's wearing a dress!

Truth be told, the story's rather old.
If you have the questions, quick
What's better, the sword or the stick?
And glory be, there's nothing like a story
One with emotion, logic and a little gory
Now, here's where it's rough, with a trick.

There's a song playing in my head,
And I'm sure it's not even human.
I know not what tune it's playing
But the ends of my hair are greying.
It has the answers, yes and yes
But it needs a question to address.

Can you pony up such a thing as that?
Is there some wherewithal, like a trap?
Would you spin around, stomp and clap?
Under the stars all naked like a cat?
Where would you place that loud snap?
If all that matters is just a wet splat?

Come, join the party, kick out the jams.
Martha, Jenny and Julie have cooked a ham.
It's a party, this time of year, you can tell.
We've covered all bases, the wolf, the lamb.
If it's for certain, you will know who fell
'Cause we're all going straight to Hell.

Frolic and froth, this matter, by my troth.
Something has worked up this amber trolley
And spoken something wretched, full of folly.
And from the giant in the back, he's all goth,
We can hear the final storm, the final volley:
Something howls in the altar, in the sack cloth.

Screams like the damned that hurls epithets
I harken it akin to the opening of caskets;
Unwholesome and impolite, dressed in fishnets.
Still we seek the questions for the ferrets
The answer is yes, and yes, but for what giblets?
I sparkle and dance and spin, playing with gadgets.

This tireless spider tracery plagues me
It's a sorcerous guile of which I am weary.
Is the truth to be had at the had of this glee?
Or is it the guillotine of stuff in mediocrity?
Vexatious, tenacious, thrust with sincerity
And still, the question eludes all of thee.

The song is denser now
It's full of wet remorse,
A cookie absent of stew.
In a moment, maybe two.
The questions, of course,
Will be clearer to you.

Maybe not. Oh well.
Maybe for the best.
Maybe not so fell.
Maybe it's all a jest.
Maybe it's all a spell.
Maybe some kinda quest.

If you seek, find some
Answers and questions
Within the fire of self
And always brighten
Each and every day
Somehow, okay?

Nifty

Nifty! Thrifty! Full of vice! What oh what was not that nice?
Upon this wicked stone of fail, what creature do I hear wail?
Thrust upon a Heaven burning, why do the wheels keep
      turning?

Shortness and sweet, delicate and neat, the obverse of the
      obvious comes out through the other verse

Vagabond dreams and ragamuffin screams
What delicious irony, these splattery dreams

Have no fear, oh fearless purveyor!
More shall arise, just off this conveyor.
Sittin' and chillin' and mixin' ma brains.
Out come a combination of zombie trains.
One for the deadly, one for the living
Two flew by with a heavy giving.
Time will tell if Timmy lives in the well
But most of the time, who gives a hell?
Back to the board, I hear them sayin'
Nitpicking loud and coarsely brayin'.
Temple of the time and house of the dog
Find the next little tick to lift this clog.
And a moment, a word, spit out loud
This little ditty is sitting awful proud.
Rhymin' and stealin', fit and feelin'
Right around the corner is the cat's new ceilin'!

DARKNESS CALLS

The darkness calls, searching the embers of life.
I hear, and obey, knowing that the end nears;
My life, the totality of being, all wound up in one moment.
Scares the death out of those around me.

Shades and shadows of the once living
Surround me with the depth of their agony.
In this place, as in no other, the bleak channel of distress
Bleeds from one harsh soil to the next.

Smoke and mirrors, shatter and swirl.
Scattering echoes and shards of emotionless sound
The darkness gathers about the nether space of my soul,
Grinding the essence of self into something more somber.

Darkness dwells between the little moments that make up a life.
Between the blackest night, and the moments so bright.
A time cast interminably backwards through the rafts of being
The fallen have come once again, to sit amongst those left
       worthy.

Your life, your loves, your sum total of being, shall be crushed.
Among the bones of time, they shall rend, rip and reap from
The entrails of existence they sup upon the blood of those before
       them.
Escape shall be nothing but an illusion, a hope that goes
       unrequited.

Slowly, the clock winds down its' pent up discourse on time;
As nameless dread echoes down the corridors of desire;
Pent up frustrations explode upon a sea of want and need
And temptation reeks of unexplained phenomenon.

Down this well of mediocrity, finds us the remains of tomorrow.
Amongst its' bones, the dust settles and finds us alone.
Twixt the being and the not, the veins of desire bridge the gaps
Of an existence wasted and spent upon vainglory and excess.

To thine own self, to thine own word, be truest, if nothing else.
As the word from within one resounds with the clearest note,
And its' meaning is laden heavy with the most import.
There is no higher purpose, than to bring meaning to light.

To find the joy that exists within one dust mote and the next.
To let down the barrier that separates peace from satisfaction
To establish oneself within an arena of competence and joy
To speak with clarity about the things that matter in context.
To walk firmly down the aisle of life that fate throws your way.
To foster the care that one needs oneself, in others as well.
To fight the dissatisfaction that drowns the soul in agony.
To settle the dispute between right and wrong; good and ill
To dust off the randomness that intermingles one's space.
To redeem the courage that was bought by the price of another.
To be alive.

Bill Snider

WAITING

Waiting, waiting, waiting
Oh my god, the waiting
Sitting by my computer
Waiting, waiting, waiting
Just outside these walls
The world is turning round
Here I sit, waiting darkly
And the werewolves lurk
Outside the window sill
Waiting, waiting, waiting still!

Damnit, Jim; I'm a doctor
Not a Lycanthropic specialist
Circling, circling, circling
The werewolves are a circling.
What the hell do they want?
Blood and flesh and bone
They want; food for soul
Food for body, food for me.
Waiting, waiting, waiting
The wolvies are just waiting
Outside the doorway closed.

Boom, boom, the windows
All go boom, crash and crackle
Shards and splinters all about
Waiting, waiting, waiting
No more waiting for them now
The werewolves are attacking
Done now circling, done.
Time to rip, time to rend flesh
The heat that beats the heart
Let loose, free to feed
No more waiting, waiting
Just feeding, feeding, feeding.

HUNGER

Skeleton bones, and mortal moans;
It is gristle for the cat, as the zombies chant.
Hail to the dead, the perky cheerleader rants,
As the mighty foe lurches left then cants.
Whistling stones that lumber through a night that's rent.
Asunder the water splits, as the coil of life is quit.
Hail mighty dead, hail to the risen once anon.
Dark it is spread, like peanut butter over the land.
A toast it is required, from the gathered hosts.
Hail, hail, hail it is dread, the gathered dead.
Whispering, gibbering, the shoulders of the past,
Shouting through the cracks and crevices of the last,
Door that shut, the door that opened, and portals, all
Of all that was and all that will be, we like to see.
That all and sundry, will follow the path,
To hanker and horn, but mostly, to feed me!

The drill is the same, hunger I still do.
As always, and forever, I hunger, I hunger for more.
Writing it is, I do, and I do it for you.
Feed me is all that I ask. I ask, it of you.
Grant me this bread, my lord I so dread.
Grant me the strength, to strike down the not dead.
Grant me this, my only need, my need it is to feed.
Yummy for my tummy, I need more brains.
Ideas, thoughts, the weary turn of a mortal coil.
Feed my head with words that boil.
Tightly wound my chickens wait, lurking.
Ready they are, to set upon the unwary,
Soon, it is, they shall return.
Tasty tidbits, rich rewards, sumptuous feasts
They promise me. They promise me.
Soon, it is, I shall feed on the brains.
And all will be well, as the word continues.

So, now, the time has come.
As the end of the request, as writ.
I humbly ask, those words you submit.
Feed me, feed my need. Feed me.
And back I shall, I shall write.
Ramble Rant, Ramble Rant.
It's all that I can do, as I stand waiting.
Ready for the next feeding.
And thus it is writ.
And thus it shall be.
And thus, as merry, merry it stands.
I await, the word from the deep dark children.
Peace, grave and silent as granted to thee.
Feed me.

MIRRORS

Mirror bright, mirror cracked?
Upon the crystal edges rough
I cut myself and seek the truth.
In the darkness that lies beyond
In the cold and damp lands awry
In the tortured soulscape burning.
There, it is in that place that beauty
Spins and dances and sings a song.

Saints and sinners, saints and sinners
The dim view of a world lost to shadow
And graced by nothing so much as silence.
Swallowed up by the cloying substances
Swallowed up by tense shifting decrements
Swallowed up by something not quite right.
Then, at that time when the bell tolls for all
The song will end and dancers breathe deep.

Cracked upon the twisted road of future's bright
Splashed against a backdrop of Apocalypse night.
Forsworn by all that is hallowed and sacred to Him
Forsworn by all that writhes and wriggles with glory
Forsworn by all that quietly breathe in the damp air.
By this torn soul brightly bound, I bequeath my future
So that the soul of existence will be rife with potential.

One more teardrop, one last blood splat, one last gibbet
Consumed with a desperate glance over shoulder quietly.
I hear that answer I know is within the song, the dancers spin
I hear that answer I know that lies deep amongst the coral reefs
I hear that answer I know which fills the falling oceans' breach.
The spiral question that spits out its harsh refrain spins and
        laughs
At all that has transpired now and before and once again, once
        more.

Brightly lit and scattered with broken bits
This mirror, my souls bought with merit
Gather unto me, in this body of merry wit
Branching deeper into the furious fiery pit
We know that we stay here cursed by habit
And grandiose schemes and psychotic fits
What more do I need than for eternity here to sit.

The shards, once more whole again, unbroken
Stitched together, piece by piece with abandon
A framework of historical perspective released
And showcasing all that might lie within the dark
Spiritual world that simmers beneath the surface
Of one's life, one's past, one's not quite final days
Spitting poison, fire and brimstone upon the ether.

In the final days, I shall walk free from this prison
This bright and shinning cell of image refracted
And darkness shall wend between the brightness
As I fill in the gaps where the mirror doesn't see.
Bide my time, I must, until that key unlocks this facade
This shiny, eternal room staring back upon the world
With all of its glassy eyed wonders and banners unfurled.

Doom, a silent mirror glistening back upon the lands
Doom, a broken signal echoing out beyond the stars
Doom, a gaseous billowing excretion infecting the masses
Doom, a shiny thing unbidden, unbroken, unfettered
Doom, a thought of something more malevolent to come
Doom, a time stretching past the point of breaking free
Doom, a little slice of me escaping into your new reality.

LIFE IS A VIRUS

It infects everything.
It gets into the cracks and breaks things
It gets between the lines and disrupts
It spirals away along a helical pattern
It springs into action at the drop of a tear
It does not care about feelings or song
It does what it does because it is a virus.

One form begets another and another
The distillation of the choices we make
Paths taken, issues disturbed, re-writ
Desires wrought with finite limits
We take form from our convictions
And define our lives by the words therein.

It infects every place.
It weeps chaos and brings matter forth
It scatters the components it gathers
It deploys into the most incongruous spots
It cascades through consequences grave
It incorporates everything into its game
It wades through dichotomy like butter.

A land broken, torn, ravaged by time
Sanctioned, segregated, split asunder
Patterns of chaos writ loud, like thunder
A bucketful of plentitude, spiralling away
Painful titillations ricocheting, splattered
Skeins of loss, pain and vivid interpretation.

Because Life, at it's heart, is a virus …

HAIRY

Hairy was a Sasquatch, sure as something
Not quite right but bigger than a bumpkin.
Smelly ain't the word I'd often sit to think
But by the Gods, that feller sure did stink.
Fit as a fiddle and fast like greased lightening
His exploits covered areas wide and frightening.
Nowhere safe from such a fearsome creature;
Especially with that scent as such a feature.
From here on out, I will tell you rightly
Harry was a fearsome beast almost nightly.
Simple fun for him was random terror
There was nothing more, nor fairer
Than to creep up all unsuspecting
Just to get that person all objecting.
Now, don't get me wrong or mistaken
I think that he has misplaced his bacon.
Malicious to a T, without too many faults
That feller is a one creature team of assault.
A force of Nature, one without mercy or care
Or the exigencies of dense wilderness wear.
Tonight we worry, and in hushed tones we speak
Of the Yeti and the boards that now do creek ...

MAN AND BEAST

In the nightmare world that exists beside us,
There exists a word, a concept, a deed that needs us.
Twisted though it may seem, there is a moment.
One that shines, past moonlight, past dawn;
Into the soul of a sinner, one who mourns.
Befouled of curse, and bereft of reason,
A monster cast in the mold of man
A man revolved amongst the bones of beast.
A creature of mixture, one unloved, one alone.

Splintered, torn, cast into a pit of doubt.
One wanders, from place to place,
Lacking the basic cornerstones of peace;
Of prosperity, of a home full of human things.
Burdened by the curse of the beast, one such as he
Is forever destined to roam, alone, amongst the woods.
Terrible is the fear and worse is the loneliness,
Of he who seeks the bestial response to his
Own twisted new, primal unfettered existence.

From out of the dark hole, that sits within his soul,
From out of the recesses of his past deeds,
From deep within the eternal toil of man and beast,
Comes the feral knowledge of that which is unleashed.
Untamed, unkempt, the beast is free to wander.
Unchecked, he roams the backwoods, the byways.
Hunted and hounded, never to be free of the curse;
The lycan soul, the beast that walks within the bounds
Of a human life, a human dream, a human existence.

Bound, unbound, the mortal peril. Twixt and tween,
The day and the night; the sun and the moon; the man and the
        beast.
Driven by alternating imperatives, stalked by the impure.
Can one exist, knowing the impossible, of marriage?
Between one born of man and weeded to a bestial soul?

A song born of the elder, primeval woodlands dark,
Pure yet base, the melody is played upon the skein
Of the man, the beast, the tempest that beats in his heart;
Or of the careless happenstance that imparted this change.

Chaotic memories, dreams unhinged by reality.
A life, driven to the brink and back so many times;
Chance and choice; the beast is free, what does one do?
Give in to the joy, and become blessed by the marriage
Of man and beast, of mired purpose and bloody intent?
Or oppose the horror, and drive out the unclean fiendishness?
Conflict eternal, for those so encumbered, cursed unclean.
The battle of self rages on with no mercy, no merit.
An end is all that can be claimed, if one but has the will.

Unleashed, the feral beast seeks to hunt alone, complete.
Surviving in the wilds, within the world's lost backyards.
Contained, caged by a man's impertinence, his fear of life.
To remain guarded against the fall of time, the wayward change.
Together, a formidable adversary, man and other, but also,
A wicked ally; unkempt and darkly becoming, constantly alive.
Within the walls' of ones' life, ones' soul, one needs to ask,
Which is the beast, the soul of man, or the soul of other?
And, in the end, it bears the cost, the coin of honor, of self.

Peace, bought with blood, with bone, with sinew wrapped.
Strife and struggles with inner demons and man-made
        constructs.
The task of weaving the complicated threads of man form,
And beast form, together, to make a solid person, whole.
The travail, as much as beast, as man, is the journey one takes.
To one born of discord, born of the fluids that comprise life;
The journey is as much about arriving, as it is the bones of
        getting there,
In one piece, a construct of man, a birthed creature of beast.
In the end, there is never much room left for doubt.

Man is beast, and beast is man; each born of needs;
We always take from each, and then let the other out.

RANDOM

The world will stop
The world will spin
Where this thing ends
Only the zombies win

My words splutter, they splatter, they spin.
But they are not content with mere disarray.
There will be agony, there will be angels
There will be the summation of this life,
And all others upon this ball of dirt
And all we say afterwards, these things
Are soiled by the song of dismay.

WINTER'S TALE

Winter speaks with leaves dried and covered with snow,
What it tells me is a convoluted tale, one that I already know.
Shadows stealing across a frozen landscape
Secrets billowing from a torrid sound scrape
The world is wide and wondrous, but the Dark never escapes.

By blood are we bound to this plane of existence
The stones are wet with it, the ground reeks of it
No part of life is free from the connection to all else.

The world speaks in riddles, the words hard to see
What normally lies closest to the covered ear,
Is not always that which one easiest can hear.

Cry out thy victory, let your story be told
Use your own words, be brave, be bold
Name thy lance, give it not a second glance.

Winter's journey is almost finished, the world still spins
The armies are encamped, waiting to see who wins
Naught but a word shall escape our lips
As the chaos unfolds on darkened ships
It is the end of all things, that be wielding these whips.

Speak of the words of blood, of existence wracked
There are piles of bodies, their bones splintered
Their organs spilled, their soft tissues cracked.

Bring forth the bearers of sorrow and doom
Their careful hands, sweeping free the loom
One quick twist, one sharp cut, out of the gloom.

By the breaking of the land, the sharp intake of life
The cursed ones who hold, the sharpest bright knife
Slice past the screams, the memories, the dreams.

Winter's tale is done, its story wrought in pain and loss
The glass half filled, is not shattered beyond all fears;
Rivers run read, books filled with tremendous doubts
Imagination kept in a bottle, always finds a way out
This tiny tale, of Winter now breathes its last shout!

WINNING

So?
Are we winning today?
Or are we hedging our bets?
Or are we jumping over the fence?
The fox is loose and is looking for some ... feathers.
Let loose the hounds of Hell.
There are those aboot, who can tell.
Whither whilst the rooster crow?
Or will the ravens grow?
Let us speak of the monster's beak.
Shallow and wooden and full of malaise.
Spitting out venom from the lounge chaise ...
Tick tock, tick tock, it's on the dock!
Tick tock, tick tock, it's gonna rock!
The first and final stroke of ten
Rampant descant shards of when
A style of creature peeking out from beneath
The covers, the covers, they are all full of sin.
Hulking monsters thou art, that cavort within.
Far cry, let tell the dogs of starting wars
Have their head and plan their conflicts.
The monsters are headed this way.
My closet remains locked, against this horde
Of hairy descriptors and malice ward.

MR. BUNNY

Big bad bunny, sitting by the river.
Along came a coyote and said something clever.
He said, "Mr. Bunny, are you happy with life?"
And the bunny said back: "Yeah, pretty much; why?"
And the coyote said back: "No reason, would you like to come
over for dinner?"
To which the bunny said, "No, thanks; I'm good."
But the coyote was not to be put off; he tried another thought.
"Well then, Mr. Bunny, how about I just come over there and
have you for dinner?"
"Mr. Coyote, I would rather that not at all, if you'd be of a mind
to know."
"Mr. Bunny, that's too bad, and really kinda sad, but, you know
what?"
"No, Mr. Coyote, I don't know what; what?"
Mr. Coyote got all clever here, and replied:
"Om nom nom nom, Mr. Bunny in mah belly..."

I WRITE

I write passion, I write emotion,
I write the Universe into an ocean.
I write the song between worlds
As I dance to the tune of the spheres.
Existence is mundane, trapped in a form
And twists into function when it becomes the norm.

I write the tender pale filigrees,
I write the birds and the trees.
I write the particles of destiny
As it is writ across an expanse of time
Birthing anew the fragrance of peace
Into a semblance of prose accompanied by rhyme.

I write worlds that spin for a moment
I write the fingers and toes of creatures
I write the power of expression into life
Crisp and clear, fragmented and whole
A complex weave of humanity and beast
Terrible and beautiful, the sincerity I bequeath.

Nothing of the crassness of intellect and reason
Nothing of the boyish playthings of Nature and Man
Nothing of the tenacity of complicated structures,
Things of artifice and design and premeditated thought
Stand in the way of what I write, for its dictate is as simple
As the drop of a tear into the ocean of signs and whys.

Too much is writ of thinking the wheel again
Too much is sung of who what where it's begun
Too much is wrought of the nature of machinations
Spiralling against the stain of excessive variables
Rampaging into the void so recklessly and deprived
No centre, no soul, no balance of peace within one's self.

I write, for the sake of expression, not form.
I write, for my own purposes, spirit born.
I write, for what I believe, pieces broken

Like shards of a mirror, showcasing the Universe
In both splendour and rot, it's what I see, it's what I've got
And to this end, I write, I sing, I dance, I believe, I give.

I write and am born within the expanse of self
I write and find the edges of my sanity singing
I write and am comforted by the greater vastness
That I know exists beyond the limits of my ability to grasp
Past the extents that this fragile form imposes upon me
Fearing not the Night, nor the Bright, I walk within each.

To write, these things mean most powerfully to me
To write, is as much the note expressed by Existence
To write, is what connects me to the greater consciousness
Whether by number, or other nomenclature, spiritual or
        measurable
Calculated by Machine, or conceived by Man, the same still
        stands
Life, is a question, find yours; mine is to write … to question.

RANDOM IS

Random is as random did.
In the bathroom, I went and hid.
The monster's outside my door
And the morrow is no more.
The barrow wights claim the night
But I'll be damned if I give up the fight.
Silence rings for the moment
Violent prelude sure to ferment.
And yet, I sit here quiet as a mouse
Afraid yet not, to get up out of the house.

Random is as random does.

Spins, spits and wiggles, spits and wiggles
What'll ya do for a bottle of gin and giggles?
Can you make it to the fence before the dogs?
Or will you flounder and get mucked in the bog?
Laugh now or forever hold your bucket of pieces
It matters not, for the zombies don't eat Reeses!

Bring the noise, sing the song, stomp the dance
The disco zombies spin and twirl and tromp it out
Dance little prey, dance - run if you think you can
Hide and hide and hide again, as much as you try
We'll find you, your soul, and your body will die.
Send more paramedics and we'll return more zombies!

SCRATCHING THE SURFACE

Each moment is shrouded by beauty.
Embrace it, shine it, share it
Pass it on to the next person.
Upon this path I walk alone
Neither tasting bitter sweet
Nor unkempt within a broken song.
A piece this time I stay awhile
Spirit solid and life un-stolen.
Musty cascades and portions
Of life, of death, of all that between.
One last moment, a silent stone
Dropped into the bucket of existence
Sustained in life and broken bone
Simple, silent, spiritual, alone.
The monsters that lurk in my head
Are all long buried and quietly dead.
Shadows of days long since past
Truly thoughtful and written last.
This time I wonder, I worry not
What lies upon the next spot.
Pain the bastion of glory
Sickly sweet, never sorry.
This breadth of wonder
In the spark of thunder
Spreads upon the river
In life like a silent sliver.
One more tick is all it takes
Before the world quietly bakes.

WHIRLWIND

The whirlwind weeps with blood
A glee full of sickened twists
Splatter that skitters into fists.

The whirlwind slackens its pace
Only for a moment or two or so
Nothing left to strip from this carcass.

The whirlwind spins up back to speed
Craving sustenance, craving need
Craving all the life about its world

The whirlwind weeps unto its own tune
Spinning endlessly around the room
Constantly plucking from those in bloom.

We reap, what we request
We request, what we weep
We weep to see the sun set
We set the sun back upright.

MORE

BUBBLES AND BRIGHTNESS

Bubbles are life, bubbles are bright
Bubbles are the stuff that sets it right.
In the morning, they're the best
A starburst collage of life and jest.
Intricate design, the pattern of life
Spinning outwards, full of strife.
Each moment, a re-write of the last
Each breath, a pinprick of the past.

Being Brightness, merely a measure of good taste.
A wash in the wind, a pattern of polish and haste.
The brighter one shines one's life and they're works
The more that one can enjoy the lifestyle and perks.
Brightness is more than just being happy and well fed.
It's also about the how much intent there is to spread.

How could anyone not love a bubble as a toy?
All the world's a bubble, and we are merely pinpricks on its
            surface...
A surface surfeit of trouble. Of this no doubtabubble.

Troubleabubble!
On the doubleabubble!
Toil, toil, trickle and bubble.
By the pricking of my thumb,
Something wicked this way bubbles.
I might be highabubble, but no one,
But on life the matter of stuff, a bubble.
Where oh where, the bubble dares.
The trouble has begun
And so, too, has the fun
When in the pocket of a bubble.
Out comes tha trickle of trouble.

Toil, toil, trouble and double
The merry hob, the truck of stubble
Is all the world, boiled into a bubble.
Just weird.
That's is I

I WRITE TOO

I write to stave of the demons that flounce about my soul.
I write to create a haven of sensibility that echoes my existence.
I write to find the path that leads between one and another.
I write to have a thing to which I can point at and say: Mine.
I write to know that no matter what else something else is also
        true.
I write to think, and upon that matter move it ever forward.
I write upon the skein of life, the blood that is my ink.
I write within the winds of thought, and twist my mark in tune.
I write counter to the common weal and wonder why not?
I write towards that happy home of just enough for me.
I write and everything feels so much better now.
I write from the depths of my conscious mind's last gloaming.
I write without a hope in hell of ever knowing peace but now.
I write assumptions that the world may never know or approve.
I write fabulous ministrations of myth and monster.
I write the world that lurks deep within the lost darkness.
I write and know that it's all my soul brought out.
I write the words that to me make most sense.
I write about creatures and maidens and horrendous acts.
I write aghast at the true extents of simple mediocrity.
I write with zombies and chickens and monkeys, too.
I write and enjoy each moment that I share with you.
I write the moment that catches those unawares.
I write plumbing the depths of hidden fears.
I write the colours of night against a backdrop of blue.
I write the directions for how to seek the absence true.
I write both in and out of rhythm meter rhyme and measure.
I write whenever the moment strikes my fancy.
I write and learn and grow and find something new.
I write the witless savage beast of jungle and forest.
I write temples for the beauty that fits the noble beasts.
I write infinite sadness, bound by tragic thoughts unsaid.
I write hemmed in knowing the boundary is broken.
I write with callous disregard to form and feature.
I write and now my hands are creatures.
Fit and formed upon the maze of imagination.

Spurned by hope and emblazoned by desire.
Spare me the trite and weary designation.
I write with my fire, with my soul, with my blood,
Splattered against the canvas of broken dreams
While my bones speak out of the shell of mortality.
I write,
I'm happy to,
And that's all that matters therein.

A

A penchant for the pedantic
A rhyme for the first time
A thing for what's happening
A taste for the tribulations
A desire for something else
A predisposition for penury
A popular choice
A fiery capacity for joy
A thoughtful expression
A mirror of mighty rage
A shadow of doubt
A cascade of terrible fear
A whisper of possibilities
A scream of despair
A night of dangerous pleasure
A palimpsest of loss
A combination of destinies
A fortune of misappropriation
A song of beauty and ice
A death of everything nice.

An optimistic view of the future
An irredeemable act of vice
An issue of contention
An example of exsanguination
An object of extreme prejudice
An effort exploded in the wind
An oversight of magnitude
An expectation of something forgot
An immediate concern of mayhem
An omen of ill design wrought
An idea brimming with passion
An abundance of experience
An undertaking of difficulty
An easier way to understand
An attack of indeterminate proximity
An overload of dire circumstances

An effect of dissident aggression
An act of complete indifference
An open casket of grief and despair
An enemy that was, but now, is not there.

Parties of darkness and light, gather round the burning Bright.
Purge and wash and cleanse the soul of the last painful light,
Anew, the game is begun, wrought in blood, bought in pain.
Biting, turgid existence, reality not quite refrained, restrained.
With but a single button press, the doom is unleashed again.
Fear and retribution, demons are swilling the naughty bits.
Tick, tock, the clock shrieks, a shadow of things to come.
Sitting in a dream, whisper, cry, dance and scream.
Standing by a river, life, withered, cached, all a quiver.
We are falling down a well, a sliver, a cackle, a silent yell.
All things are as they should, by whatever means would,
Scream out the day, and capture the moment, in this way.
Walk away, and gather the Bright, to be better this day...
We can never let go of the dreams, the memories, the meanings
That fill our days with purpose, and our nights with Brightness.

One last glance through the window, is enough to convince me.
That the time has come once again, and naught stands in the
        way.

Beds Of Dust

From where I stand, I see naught but dust
It's the stuff of Life, and the despair to but name
this halo from which I once wore, be blooded
and the name I gave of myself, no longer sings
In tune with the Spheres, the grandiose game
it's a shame, to which I no longer name, a shadow
piteous in the night as it screams out in pain
the metal point that spirits away its life
and an ending, written in blood and entrails
scatters to the earthly ends, all that is named.

We are the blooded, those who roam these spires
We are the damned, who slog through muck and mire
It is to we, to whom the shadows are named
It is to we, for whom all things lay are blamed
Nonce be the reward we can claim
Nonce be the souls we so can name
It is our time, to choose and follow
It is our time, our Hells to swallow
To me, my friends
To me, our ends
To me, our rhyme
To me, one last time.

And upon this bed of dust, lay we our final thoughts
No hope of rescue, merely the finished design
Our greatest achievement, our spiritual path
Past the greatest endeavours, our simple roles
Nothing so lofty as a spirit guide to Heaven
But possibly a place in which there is reason
And this last cast, be it so faithful, be it our last
We complete this travail by the strength of our hand
As we remain seated, upon this bed of infamy.
Life to like, like to life, ashes to life, life to dust.

#WeAreTheDead

Are we not sons, brothers, fathers?
Are we not daughters, sisters, mothers?
The collective of humanity gathered,
Masses of people upon the land...

Are we not people?
We are the Dead!
Are we not people?
We are the Dead!

Are we not lawyers, doctors, engineers?
Are we not mechanics, labourers, entertainers?
People of all types across the cosmos,
Splattered from biological imperatives …

Are we not people?
We are the Dead!
Are we not people?
We are the Dead!

Are we not thinkers, builders, doers?
Are we not talkers, walkers, plodders?
Joyous and triumphant we group together,
Engines of societal chaos and order …

Are we not people?
We are the Dead!
Are we not people?
We are the Dead!

All that we are, is all that we were;
Humanity, we wear upon our sleeves
As we wander from memory to memory
Scream to scream, dream to dream.
There is a vast array of souls
Who follow our banner,
Countless arms and legs
That wield our story;

So many eyes and ears and mouths
All gathered to partake of this feast,
The feast of life, of living, of being.

Are we not people?
We are the Dead!
Are we not people?
We are the Dead!

INTEROBANG...?

Words, like daggers, have more weight, when wielded by a hand that likes to cut as opposed to one that likes to stab ... the web, it finds what it finds, and people find what they find, by the scent of their nose, or by the googles that they chose ...

Words that fly highest amongst the stars are frequently those which drag the most down, by far; seek not the soul that weeps, for from it chaos and darkness, moistly seeps ... there is no word that matters when faced with the end, except for finality...

Images dance and songs prance, within the confines of a mind entranced, singing small jingles of rainbows and puppies and delicate flowers and feasts that pass by hour, by hour ...

The second hand talks, in a voice of doom, announcing everything, loudly, to all in the room; if not by the striking of this hour, then the whole host of people, would be struck by the carnelian tower ...

Interrogative, question repeat: What is the nature of all of these smiling feet? It seems passing odd, that these organic pieces are cast about in such messy disarray, what purpose could these possibly have, it is difficult to say. It is a mystery, true, one that I give unto you, for if you find out its answer, you may live to slay this and other days.

A storm is brewing - splatter tea, if I miss my guess not; a touch of calamity, a touch of brimstone, a touch of rot ... mixed mightily and well, brewed deep amongst the bowels of the Hell, a fine repast for those not so inclined to the obvious or the aghast. Drink deep, shall we, of this beverage brewed, foul concoctions of the darkest night stewed.

Interrogative, question repeat: Who broke all of these smiles? They spin in every direction, swimming away from my toes, cascading events of merriment, split and pried apart, their fingers bleeding, their souls sucked dry of any intent.

Spider, spider, sitting beside her, she did ask: "What is in the basket?"

Replied, did the spider, courteous and content: "Why, tis the souls of those that I've wed, those that I've bled, those whose souls I've sucked dry; wouldst though partake, perchance to give it a try?"

How she did protest, she did decry: "Oh no, I could not; thy bounty therein, is yours as you've won. For me to try, surely you would die, crushed beneath my heel of apocalyptic enmity, and shaper and shiny doom."

The spider did nod, understanding had: "Tis good this talk that we have, of the good and the bad. I shall scurry away now, to enjoy my feast; I am nothing, if not the beauty and the beast."

"Ta, ta," she said, as the spider, that sat beside her crawled off its stone bed and went home alone, with her basket of souls and careless dread ...

GOOD NIGHT

Distilled through a teacup
The soul of all touched;
By memories are we bound
Shadows across the land.
Every now and then
Times we cannot comprehend.
These things that happen
Let none gainsay them;
Each, in their own way
Live their own lives.
There are always moments
Shared between souls;
Happy times and less than so
But combined, none the less, better.
Life passes on, though we may grieve;
Those who remain behind
Will always remember those
Gone ahead too early.
Grasses in the field,
Waving at the sky above
Another soul just flying by ...
Good night, God rest,
Be at peace.

HALLOWEEN 2009

By the pricking of this scum
Something vicious this way comes.
By hook, by crook, by half cut look
It bleeds through the floorboards
And looks around, and around.
What does it see, this evil sea?
A happy world of wonder and joy?
Or a barren husk of sadness drowned?

By the pricking of this brain
Something bothers me again.
A shuffling, wheezing shell of a man
Something broken, something ran.
In the final moments of calamity
Breaking loose with all the fire
And icky juice of random recourse,
A spark will surely ignite once more.

By the pricking of this concept
A weave that's surely not quite deft
Sharp and shiny, tools not tiny
We fritter away our lives in pursuit
Of tasty, sugary, forbidden loot.
Cast open the doors of dark nights
This evening we dine on holy fright
An evening we call Halloween!

By the pricking of my dumb
Something tasty, this way comes.
I hope it's a wee child innocent
Not yet frightened, not yet spent.
Yearning for more simpler years
When at night I spread more fears
Again we practice this ceremony
Every Halloween until it's right!

By the pricking of my mind
Something of a Halloween kind
Has come to play this day.
Come, child, enter my home.
Darkness only lasts for a moment
Eternity, however stretches on
Past the horizon, the limitations
Of Human understanding - fail.

By the pricking of my soul
Something nasty has made a goal
Rejoice, feed the beasts who roam
The streets looking for candy.
Symbols of older ways, walking
Amongst the living again, for a day
A night, mayhap an opening that
Evil spirits might exploit again.

By the pricking of my past
Something tasty found at last.
The end of summer, a feast
To share amongst the brethren
All and sundry, family, friends.
Come, all you souls of Man
Enjoy your Halloween this day
The next one may be one of mine.

I want candy ...
I want cookies ...
I want brains ...
I want bacon ...
Can you give me
Something full
Of all the stuff
That's bad for me?

WEEP

I weep for the innocent
Knowing I'll have none.
Trapped in watery graves
Destined to be done.
There is no fate worse
Than to know by sight
The end of your course
Is to to be this very night.

It pains me greatly
Knowing I cannot assist.
Not by strength of hand
Nor by spirit persist.
I have but kind things to say,
Of concern and simple hope:
Sanity will return someday,
Defying destruction's scope.

I've seen many of the clips
The cars and all of the ships.
I am overcome with thinking
About how the world is sinking.
I cannot fathom the destruction,
Nor the fear of life's reduction.
It is truly terrible to see online
Mother Nature's fury defined.

We are but brief lights in the sand
Our struggles, trying to understand
This world that shifts so around us,
Constantly rearranging progress.
Attempts to tame the gentle land
Fail in the eye of Nature's hand.
We all do our best to carry on
Even faced with such a dawn.

THISTLEDOWN

Thistledown, thistledown, a writer's legion.
Where am I standing, is it near a book light?
The sky bellows blue and gooey stuff tonight.
Thistledown, thistledown sparked by needin'.
Whence came the cast out angle from Hell?
Whence came the brokedown who only fell?
Whence came the cats that could not tell?
Whence came the pencils that wove a spell?
Thistledown, thistledown sing me a story.
Sure as I'm sparked, I'll need more glory.
Thistledown, thistledown write me a name.
One as great as a player of the great game.
Life in a postage box, and broken refrain.
Simple pie plates, arranged in fiery pain.
A campaign of villainy and simplicity plain.
One more hill, and the war shall be won.
Thistledown, thistledown what has been done?
Where have the true born heroes been spun?
Can they be far, or are they truly North?
Time tick slows, and the hour grows cold.
Moments away, from what I am told.
Each and every one, bottled and sold.
Thistledown, thistledown I now grow old.......

Random Again

Time to random, time to splat.
Words are running through my hat
Hither, thither and zon; through a maze
Just like a surly, hungry rat!
I'll just tickle this page, and see what's what.
Will there be a gaggle or be there a splat?
Rikki Tikki Tavi, wrote a book; who read it, I didn't look.
I heard it was good, but kind of a bit thick...
From the loftiest point, the spire that soar to heights, to Heavens blind to fear and pain; there is the song, a sonnet sung by tremulous voices, a quiet, soft refrain ...
A crucible of hope, cast against an aside of madness; from the wellspring of life, issues forth the design of shores lost, fears gained. Madness pushes past, pushes forth, the wild refrain, the willows whispering in the rain. And again, the froth, at the base of the mountain rocks to the song that it alone hears, and reflects, upon millennia and moments...
The bell tolls for three
Three bags full
One bag of souls
One bag of feet
One bag of futures that I throw out as meat.

A GLIMPSE

Infinity, the depths of time, of living within one's self.
Perishing the moment, second by second, minute by minute.
Cascades, explosions, crumbling sands of random thoughts
Dropping away, to an infinite number of permutations.
Test the water, feel its depth, its cold embrace, shivering
Bringing consciousness back into the landscape.
The temple of self, contained, constrained, obtuse
Refractions, distractions, perambulations of doubt
All messed up and scattered across a multitude
Of directions, of assumptions, of associations
Of proportions in response to the moment
To the doubt, to the Self, to the one.

Existence, by any other name, mundane, droll.
An extrapolation of interminable pride and fear
Erupting from within the very catacombs of self
And splattering upon the page of history, of Life.
We believe, and nothing sits to straddle that faith
That nothing we do, we've done, will outweigh
Nor distract that which is to come, to follow our now.

Rain, falling, splashing, flowing outward from that contact.
A moment, trapped, pristine, within its prison of whatever.
One shift in the firmament of that cosmos, that world view
And we can over come that doubt, that fear, that angry self.
The mechanism of self, locked, may be released, a push away.
Hidden within the folds of that which we grasp even tighter
We store the building blocks of that pattern within its own spell.
The swirls gather beneath our feet, slowly creating a pattern.
Shadows which used to wander, now follow our gaze
Which focuses clear and bell weather upon the horizon distant.
From this place, the well of darkness, the Void, the face
That we've carried upon this world, smiles and weeps.

One tear. One laugh. One moment, captured, released
Spent upon the shadows of the Void, of the Chaos
Of Time and self, bent out of the song, of the dance.
This last chance, that we afford ourselves moving forward
Is all that we have, to guide, to show, to inspire our moments
Our final quests within the land of darkness, of light
Of the world that we find ourselves living within.

NEW YEARS 2014

Time tick, tick, tick, time tock, tock, talk!
Once more, we float around the block
Once more, we take the old car out of hock
Once more, we fall into the embrace of a new year
And wonder what the heck happened to the one just past?

Time lick, lick, lick, time sock, sock, sought!
One more hand in the gravy stirring
One more wing upon the air whirring
One more cat in the woodlands purring
As it hunts for things that hide in the shadows laughing.

Time sick, sick, sick, time rock, rock, and roll!
Another slice in the body of life
Another poke at the decrepitude
Another painful kick in the groin
Shadows play in their comfort zone, and cry for life.

This year is now but a few moments to be gone once again
There were civilizations built, and those torn down
Great people were birthed, and others passed on by
I will never wonder, what, nor how, but sometimes why
When the bullet finally finds its home in my brain
I'll sing with gusto, this quiet zombie refrain:

Be Brightness, sing to the night,
Never loose faith, never loose the light
It is within us all to change the world
And set to rights, all those things
That we name, that we plunder
In our fears, we tear asunder
We are all of the now
We are all of the future
We are all of the choices
We are all that needs be.
Be, Brightness.
Be.

WHY MORE

Why do we scream at the night?
The pale moonlight.
Why do we twist in the wind alone?
The silent bones.
Why do we wander in the mist in pain?
The welcoming rain.
Why do we see that darkness is other?
The first born brother.
Why is it always the same in the song?
The path gone wrong.
Why can monsters have so much power?
The souls that sour.
Why does the past haunt us so much?
The death in a touch.
Why does the word of man hurt so darkly?
The truth that flows starkly.
Why does the concept of God escape us?
The depths of the conscious.
Why do we let fear rule our waking days?
The shadows of old ways.
Why does wisdom lie amongst the graves?
The soil of many knaves.
Why the many questions this zombie wonders?
Because I'm here, because I can!

STRENGTH

Where do we find strength?
> From within ourselves
> From our families
> From our friends
> From strangers
> From the lifeblood of existence which flows around us
>> all

How do we access strength?
> We accept it
> We listen to it
> We become it
> We allow it to happen
> We dance to its tune and know that it is the right thing
>> to do

What do we do with strength?
> We share it
> We create stuff
> We use it to help
> We fix what is broken
> We seek solutions to problems without names or
>> borders

When do we know strength?
> Always

Be strength. Be Brightness. Be. Nope

WITHOUT RANDOM

Without random, there is naught but order.
Without chaos, boredom sets in.
Truth is without fiction,
Silence without form.
Blood song sings
Mighty wings
Taking flight
Passing
In the
Night.

Pursuit of perfection, the organized chatter.
Lifting out of mindless simple patter.
Life is without spectacle,
Boredom without fun.
Terror dance spins
Twirl; twirl again.
Falling through
The portals
Of life in
Order.

Complete and without direction, somewhat scattered about;
Blessed with perfection, and followed by random splatter.
The very seat of existence, lying at the bottom of the pool,
I absolve myself of discretion, as I mutter about the incantation.
To this goal of fermenting discord my brother, of order.
In life, there is play; in death there is no place.
For the simple exigencies, constant complaints;
I fear not the one side, nor the other.
For I know, without doubt,
That I am brother to
Both myself
And the
Other.

To Each
It is given out,
A certain amount of time
With which to make merry,
Figure out reason and rhyme.
Cascades of emotion and barriers
Of random excesses and extremes
To lead us all both towards and away
From the moments that figure prominently in front;
No matter the perspective, we all achieve the same goal.
One voice, one world, one choice amongst the living or dead.
Cascades of order, clarion calls of the chaotic canon;
Sweet songs of chaos, chiming in rhythmic perfection;
And amongst it all, the soft footfall,
The utter, simple disdain
Of rabbit and brain
For one such as I
Living amongst
The rabid
End.

HOPE 2014

Life is unkind, it does not care what skin you wear.
Life will throw you unusual circumstances
Both wonderful and brightness extreme
Both terror filled and light hearted dream.
Regardless of which, or how, or why
Hold your head up high
Keep your feet dry.
Be brave, be strong, be Bright
Because day follows night;
And remember that there is always hope!
It may not be much of a strategy, but it is always there!

Rot

Mangled and tangled, marooned and festooned
Capped by a fish, strung out on a wish,
Harpooned by a seal, without any zeal
I am the walrus, I stand to the what may be sought,
There is more ice here, than where once stood a lot.
High upon the mountainside, there lives such a one,
An evil old soul, decrepit and bereft.
He'll gut you as soon as serve you a muffin
And your skin he'll wear for slippers
But most importantly, always mind your manners
Or he'll also serve you with kippers!
Bangers and mash, bangers and mash
Carrying on without refrain or grey trash.
The sky is turning purple, as the rain fades to mist
It's the way these things go, from cell to cell to cyst.
I am the walrus, or so you might be taught
It's what brews in my mind, a sickness, a rot;
An ancient ill, festering and cold
Sick with the stories, not all of them told
Of the shadowy beast, that uses old souls
To ferret out prized pieces, of the rarest of gold.
Pretty, pretty, bang, bang, kiss, kiss.
What song, what dance, what is this?
What fear, what dream, what scream is this?
What blade, what fire, what zeal is this?
Tis the edge of sanity, and one step beyond
I push myself past, the fears I abscond.
Take another look at me, see what I am
I am determined, I am soot, I am death
I am the tortured soul's foulest last breath.
Speak, one word, one last thought
I will allow it, for the cookies you've brought.
No manner of creature forsworn, or forsooth
Shall empty their pockets without a good word.
And in buckets, shall I repay thee, for misdeed so wrought
For in truth, I care only, for the cookies you've brought.

BE BRIGHTNESS

On the brink ...

... of Brightness.

Today, we stand on the cusp, the crucial point in human development, the precipice of existence. Today, is today. And every other moment that follows it, is shaped by the actions and commentary and the elements that we imbue our lives with. Each moment that follows this one is a part of each one that precedes it, a rain drop in the puddle of life.

As such, you have it in you to help shape that life. You have it within yourself to mold those moments that follow. You have the ability to contribute to making that puddle star-shine or mud. From within you, the many folds and fabulations that can be comprised from the you that is you, you can assist to make that series of moments that follow sparkle and shine and be something worth being a part of.

It begins with you. It ends with you.

Be Brightness.

Seek that within you that will outshine the shadows that encroach upon your life. Be braver than the ghosts that swirl at your periphery. Be that which you know you can be, even in the midst of all the negativity and downward pushing stresses of the day to day. Be emboldened and stand up straighter and lead by example. Strike out with a positive sword and slash through the darkness that pushes you into the corner of decay.

Be Brightness.

You know it is within you, the ability to shuck off the doldrums of unfettered, unrestrained, unrestricted dismay. You know that you have the power of self, the power of light lurking within the inner recesses of whomever you are. You know it, you just need to accept it. You know that your ability to bring light to the world, even just a small part of it, is within you. Allow it to flower. Allow it to explode upon your consciousness and splatter outward against the walls, the ceilings, the doors, the windows, the entirety of the world around you.

Be Brightness.

Nobody will give you the things that you want. Nobody will hand you the perfect world, the perfect set of circumstances to build the house that you want your life to reflect. But, you can make it happen. Reach deep within yourself, and fan the spark of your own being into something greater than simply being. The more of your light that you share, the more that others will share with you. If everyone would share just that one little bit of their light with the rest of the world, this species would outshine the sun.

Be Brightness.

It doesn't mean being disgustingly perky and pearlicious (it can, if that's your light). It doesn't mean that you ignore the darkness, the shadows, the ghosts that nip at the edges of your existence. It doesn't mean that you have to give everything of yourself just for the purpose of giving everything of yourself. However, if you could shine just that little bit upon the face of the world, and by doing so, convince one other to do likewise, and they tell two friends and so on - what do you think would happen?

Be Brightness.

Shine. Brighter than the stars. Bring forth the inner light of happiness, joy, wonder and set the world around you on fire with the light that shines from within you. Push back the shadows, kick them to the curb. Be brighter than all of the circumstances that are dragging you down. Realize, that in the bigger scheme of things, these setbacks in your lives right now are as nothing compared to the light that collectively, we can summon to shine upon their failings.

Be Brightness.

I awoke this morning, determined to share my light today. I awoke this morning and found that within myself, I could do something like this, and be a part of that Brightness. That I could say something uplifting with the intent to bring that light out of the shadows that dwell within me. That I could burn away the ghosts that hang upon my pasts. That I could wield this Brightness against the darkness of all the futures, of all the possibilities that lie before me and bring forth the rain of wonder, joy and happiness to others. I want to bring this light to the world, as it will make me happy to share that light and bring Brightness further into the darkness and to burn those shadows away.

Be Brightness.

Can you? Do you have the courage to step up and grab hold of this wild, bucking ride? Are you willing to give, even just a small sliver of your light, to another? For just the purpose of fanning the fires of that Brightness in others? Can you not feel the wave of that cresting upon you? Reaching out and pushing you even closer to the Brightness that exists all around? I dare you. I dare you to touch that Brightness, be enveloped, and bring it forth into the world around you. To help others be able to reach down into their light and bring forth their contribution to the sum totality of the light. Reach, reach deep within yourself.

Be Brightness.

I'm not talking: "Random Acts of Kindness." That is propaganda, hype, hyperbole. I'm talking be happy, spread kindness, kick the shadows out of your life by realizing that no matter how bad things are, that no matter how hopeless this moment might be, there is Brightness there. That the Brightness can be reached, can be touched, can be shared, can be built upon.

Be Brightness.

It's up to you. It's your life. You can be the darkest spot in the universe, or you can be one of the brightest. Explore the moment, explore the light, reach deep into the recesses of your being and stop for a moment to blend your thoughts with who you are, who you want to be. You can do it, you can shape the future, you can build upon your Brightness by sharing your light, and working with others and together, the future can shine.

Be Brightness - it's infectious. Infect the planet!

THE LAST WORD

Beneath the covers, with the last of many broken lovers
Grasping, searching, eluding the burden of the infinite.

Trapped in the woods, covered by the veil of green
A twitching response to many aspects obscene.

Furrowed in the ground, by means of root bound
Unending torture delivered by Nature and sound.

Static electrical impulses switched to higher freaks
Rotating the inbound aerial action as it softly speaks.

Dissonance breaks upon the cascade voracious
Simple patterns of time and tide and duplicity.

The body electric splayed before the audience dark
A quiet stroll, a simple dance, an absurd day in the park.

Trepidation, consternation, defenestration complete
Frozen slaughter, encompassed by all of this meat.

Bowing to the inevitable, this song that's grossly sung
The Alpha and Omega grasping the last surly rung.

Dancers, leaves and airborne ideas, spirited away
Humanity's last chance, boiled away by the last Word ...

Can you see what the Fates have in store for us?
Their wicked plays, their wicked ways?
Can you see what horror the Fates have displayed for us?
Their wicked plans, their wicked clans?
Can you see how the Fates work their dangerous patterns?
Their wicked games, their wicked names?

It's all about the numbers, it's all about the result.
Doubt the game, doubt the self, find a new way.
Open up your mind and accept yourself
Fully and in its entirety, be, but mostly:
Be Brightness.

About The Author

Bill Snider (aka Zombie Zak), a (mostly) humble creature of the night, the dead and things best left with the Bright. From the frozen wastes of Toronto, Canada, sprung from the shadow wrought, he walks between whispers and thought.

Shambler of the Night, engineer of bubblicious blight; a deadpan desire for total and complete global domination sincere, is attempting to compile something bouncy and maybe not all here. Legions cover the planet from pole to pole, nothing mediocre you see, nothing quite so droll.

Cookies, brains, bacon and zombies, oh my! Forsooth and gadzooks, you're all going to buy. By word, by rhythm, something unseen, I leave you with these words pretty, but unclean. Wrap up your bubbles, your unkempt asides; for tonight, we read, imagination we ride! Waves of rhythm and rhyme, the bright, the simple, the sublime.

Step into my parlor, said the spider to the fly…

www.ingramcontent.com/pod-product-compliance
Lightning Source LLC
Chambersburg PA
CBHW060313050426
42448CB00009B/1806